Single-ish

31-Day Devotional
for the
Single & Single Again

by

STACY Y. THOMAS

Watersprings
PUBLISHING

Singleish: 31-Day Devotional for the Single & Single Again
Published by Watersprings Publishing,
a division of Watersprings Media House, LLC.
P.O. Box 1284 Olive Branch, MS 38654
www.waterspringspublishing.com
Contact publisher for bulk orders and permission requests.

Printed in the United States of America.

ISBN-13: 978-1-948877-85-5

TABLE OF CONTENTS

Introduction

This life is one big, beautiful dance. One moment we're dancing a beautiful solo with seamless pirouettes and dashing leaps, and the next minute we've acquired a partner to join us in this dance called life. For some, the duet ended up rhythm-less, as they discovered during the dance that someone had two left feet. For others, one partner was tap dancing while the other was dancing to afro-beats. Both dance genres make a lot of noise, but when the music is played, and the moves are danced out simultaneously, all you hear is noise, and all you see is confusion. For others, life has always been a solo dance. Just one person in a huge room where the silence is deafening, yet when the music plays, the sound bounces off the walls as they dance gracefully, yet alone.

For the next 31 days, I want to introduce you to your dance partner – the Holy Spirit. I will be your choreographer, and between the three of us, we are going to dance through this beautiful thing called the single life. So journey with me, as we uncover hard truths and hidden gems about singleness, as well as fortify ourselves with the truth, and rid ourselves of the lies that society at large has fed the masses about single life.

As your choreographer, I have extensive experience. After a marriage that ended after seven years, and a wedding for a second marriage that never took place, the Lord impressed it in my spirit to write this devotional. I understood exactly why, and I agreed with God (as if I had a choice). There are very few people who speak about singleness while they are single.

More and more, there are people who are owning their singleness and being bold and unapologetic about it, but it's not nearly enough. In most cases, the people speaking to singleness are married, and they only speak to it after they've gotten married. I believe it is because most times, those who are married struggled with singleness themselves, so they have very little to say about how to successfully live as a single person.

God commissioned me to write this book now while I am still single. I do not plan to be the poster child for singleness, and I am by no means claiming to have all of the answers, but this I know- there is a need for more tangible examples of people living single successfully. While I am not perfect, I am not ashamed of my past or current state. I am a firm believer that God does not waste pain, so He is using my experience mainly because I allowed Him to cut in and take the lead in this dance called the single life, and since He has, my life has never been the same.

So, I invite you onto the dance floor. Lace up your shoes, roll up your sleeves, pull your hair up into a messy bun because we have work to do for the next 31 days.

Grown Folks Conversation

When I was a child, I talked like a child, I thought like a child, I reasoned like a child. When I became a man, I put childish ways behind me.

Everything about who we are today can be traced back to our childhood. From the traditions we carry to the decisions we make, believe it or not, the person we are in this very moment is the sum total of our past.

Society has this uncanny way of shaping who they think we ought to be, based on their standards. Society says a person (particularly a woman) is not complete without a mate. Because of this belief, some of us have gone from childhood to adolescence to adulthood, then straight into marriage. Others went into adulthood and have yet to step into marriage. Either way, there was seldom time and space given for womanhood or manhood. Most of us were not taught how to transition from boy to man or girl to woman. All we were given was a blank canvas, which we filled with a laundry list of things we wanted to accomplish, along with unrealistic timelines based on society's standards.

With each stage of growth, we dragged our upbringing, environment, decisions, and traditions (good and bad) into our relationships, with no guidance, no mentor, no sound advice. All we were given was false information passed down from generation to generation and social media that provides a warped, unrealistic view of relationships. The worst part about this is, with all that we've picked up and dragged along the way, we left two of the most important components out-self-awareness and self-love.

In 1 Corinthians 13, Paul talks extensively about love. This chapter is called the love chapter, but I would venture to call it the "grown folks" chapter because in order to self-actualize, live, and serve at this level of love, one must be mature mentally and emotionally. Paul would agree, hence the declaration he made in verse 11 about the difference between who he was as a child and who he became as a full-grown man. In his writings, you can tell that Paul exhibited both self-awareness and self-love.

What about you? Do you have self-awareness about your past and who you are currently? Do you exhibit self-love in your actions, or do your actions exhibit adolescent behavior? Can you honestly say you've put away childish tendencies? Who shows up when things go really well or really bad, the little girl/boy in you or the grown woman/man? I ask these questions because whether we know it or not, whether single or single again, your past will shape every single relationship you have, one way or the other.

Every. Single. One.

So, on this day, let's carefully pull back the layers of who we are for real – and take inventory regarding how we show up in our own lives. Let's dissect and deal with childhood traumas, broken environments, and negative stigmas, so we can put away the childish mannerisms, motives, and mindsets that keep us from living our best life, single and satisfied.

LET US PRAY

Heavenly Father, I come to You humbly, asking You to accompany me as I travel back into my childhood. God, You know all things, for You formed and fashioned me. You knew every obstacle I would face, every traumatic experience I would encounter, and every hurt I would endure. Now God, I am ready. I am ready to face the things of my past, so I can be healed, delivered, and set free. I am ready to face the child in me so that I can transition into the person You have called me to be NOW. Help me, Lord, and give me the courage to walk through those tough places and close every door and every portal that has served as a hindrance to all You would have me to be. I thank You in advance, in Jesus' name, amen.

REFLECTION

What childish ways/attitudes/thought patterns have you
put away?

_____

_____

_____

_____

_____

_____

Are there any childish ways/attitudes/thought patterns you
are struggling with?

_____

_____

_____

_____

_____

_____

Self-Awareness & Self-Love

I Am God's Handiwork!

PSALM 139:14 (NLT)

Thank you for making me so wonderfully complex!
Your workmanship is marvelous —
how well I know it.

One of the signs of maturity as an adult is knowing who you are. A sign of maturity *and* a balanced life is knowing who you are outside of companionship. Knowing who you are and being whole before entering a relationship will save you from heartbreak most of the time. However, even in knowing who you are, sometimes heartache and heartbreak can cause you to second guess yourself and have thoughts of inadequacy.

If you've lived a little while, you've most likely dealt with relationship heartbreak or loss. If you've been single as a grown adult for some time, you may have dealt with some feelings of inadequacy about your journey and failed attempts at love as a result of those losses. My friend, you must understand that you lack nothing. Yes, you are the sum total of your experiences and environment, but as long as you have breath in your body and a willingness to do and be better, you can deal with the pain of your past (or present), so you can be better for your future. You are God's handiwork, beautiful in your own way and in your own right!

When God created you, He didn't make any mistakes. He didn't run out of "the good parts" and just give you whatever was remaining. From your hair follicles to your toenails, He created you with intentionality, and He has the person in mind who will capture your heart when it is time! You don't have to change who you are because someone else didn't appreciate you, or you think no one is looking your way. Be secure in the fact that you are the answer to someone's prayer! Know that you are beautiful, sexy, intelligent, and have a lot to offer. Use this time of singleness to love and appreciate you!

LET US PRAY

Heavenly Father, I decree today that I AM fearfully and wonderfully made! Being the perfect and intentional God that You are, You made no mistakes when You fashioned me. From the crown of my head to the soles of my feet, You strategically fashioned me the way You saw fit for Your purpose and Your glory. There is someone out there who will see me through Your eyes someday. There is someone praying for everything I have, and I declare I am the answer to someone's prayer. Until that time comes when we are united, I pray that You continue to reveal to me all You have made me to be. I want to get to know me for ME, so when I am presented to the one You have for me, not only will they know what they are receiving, but I will know as well. In addition, knowing all of who I am will open my eyes to discern the counterfeit partner. Help me to listen to that still small voice that whispers, "This is not the one," accept Your counsel, and remove myself from any relationship that was not sanctioned and ordained by You. I thank You in advance for this journey of self-discovery so I can be the best version of me for my present and my future, in Jesus' name, amen!

REFLECTION

Who are you? Answer by making "I AM" declarations:

I AM _____

_____

_____

I AM _____

_____

_____

I AM _____

_____

_____

I AM _____

_____

_____

I AM _____

_____

_____

I am God's Handiwork!

Being Content in Singleness

PHILIPPIANS 4:11 (AMP)

Not that I speak from [any personal] need, for I have learned to be content [and self-sufficient through Christ, satisfied to the point where I am not disturbed or uneasy] regardless of my circumstances.

To be content means to be in a state of peaceful happiness or a state of satisfaction. I think it's important to note that the word "state," in this context, is a noun and means to express something definitely or clearly.

One of the keys to living successfully single or single-again (after divorce) is to be content in the state you are in. It's not enough to just "be" content. Extra effort has to be put forth because singleness is not celebrated the way relationships and marriage are. As humans, we want companionship. Even in Genesis, God declares it is not good for man to be alone (Genesis 2:18).

This era of social media doesn't help. Everywhere you look, you see countless posts and pictures of couples. A lot of people are posting about their wonderful relationships (whether they are or not), marriage proposals, and random pics of just beautiful and glorious days of sheer happiness and bliss. Rarely do you see a barrage of pics of singles living their best life. Instead, singleness is often synonymous with loneliness, despair, and waiting for something better to happen (as if singleness is so bad).

Marriage, on the other hand, confirms one is desired, wanted, and deemed worthy by another person. In other words, singleness means no one wants you, but once you're engaged and married, then you actually become worth something because you are desired. Therefore, you can start living your life to the fullest.

The devil is a liar.

Being content in your singleness doesn't mean you don't desire a relationship. Being content means that in your singleness, your desire doesn't override your common sense, turning into despair and desperation. While you wait for that special someone, you enjoy your life to the fullest and take advantage of the opportunity of being single.

Here is a tough question: if you never got married or remarried, would you be okay with that? Yes, I know in Day 2, we tackled being found by that special someone, but today, we have to have an honest conversation about our will versus God's will for our lives. The truth of the matter is, everyone is not going to get married (just as everyone won't be healed on this side of heaven).

Can you find contentment in that probability? Can you live with the desire for companionship AND the possibility of that not being your story or God's will for your life? Yes, that's a tough pill to swallow, but my friend, this is what separates the mature from the immature, and the content from the discontented! This is what separates those who can only be happy for others once they've found happiness themselves from those who can genuinely be happy for others regardless of the state they are in. That's true contentment! Not there yet? It's okay. Let us pray so we can get there!

LET US PRAY

Gracious God, show me what true contentment is in You. Show me all of the benefits of being single. Give me the boldness to inwardly affirm that I am content in my singleness and the courage to outwardly declare the same. As I wait on You to bless me with who You have for me, I pray that You bring like-minded individuals into my life that are equally as content in their singleness. I cancel any and all thoughts of jealousy when I see and hear the good news of others in their relationships. Cause me to remember that someone else's season of love doesn't cancel out mine, as it is not my time yet. Until my time comes, I will celebrate others and enjoy my singleness simultaneously. If by some chance my time never comes and it is not Your will, TEACH ME, GOD, to celebrate others and to lean into You to see what You do have for my life. No matter what, I decree and declare it is going to be amazing! In Jesus' name, amen.

REFLECTION

Can you say you are truly content in your singleness currently? (Note: there is no right or wrong answer. What's important is your honesty).

_____

_____

_____

If you <u>are</u> content, what can you do to ensure you stay content until your status changes?

_____

_____

_____

If you <u>are not</u> content, why not? How will you work to change your feelings?

_____

_____

_____

_____

Are you content
in your singleness?

What's on My Mind?

Finally, brethren, whatsoever things are true, whatsoever things are honest, whatsoever things are just, whatsoever things are pure, whatsoever things are lovely, whatsoever things are of good report; if there be any virtue, and if there be any praise, think on these things.

Believe it or not, what you think determines your speech and actions. Often, we try to keep our negative thoughts hidden by making positive confessions. But we don't realize that eventually, what we think can (and in most cases, will) seep out in the way we speak and carry ourselves.

Immediately after a really bad breakup, I found myself thinking negative thoughts about myself. The very public breakup left me in a state of shock and embarrassment. There were people who secretly celebrated the end of that relationship. Others circulated vicious rumors and fabricated stories. At some point, I felt like I was starting to believe what people were saying about me.

As quickly as I found myself traveling down that rabbit hole of negativity that could've led me down a path to low self-esteem, anger, and bitterness, the Holy Spirit lovingly reached down, grabbed me, and pulled me out. It wasn't easy shaking off the wickedness that was trying to close in on me, but the power of God is amazing. As I searched the Word of God to try to arm myself with spiritual weaponry, Philippians 4:8 stuck out to me. I had to shift my thinking and change my perspective on what had taken place and challenge myself to think about what was true, honest, just, pure, lovely, and of a good report. All of those thoughts led me straight to God. Once this happened, I was able to lay all of my grievances at the feet of Jesus, and in return, the Holy Spirit helped me to decipher the things that were true, honest, just pure, lovely, and of a good report concerning me and that situation. He's so amazing like that!

This is my story. What's yours? What has happened to you that has shifted your thinking? What lies has the enemy told you? What lies have you told yourself? Please understand, you can think yourself out of negativity. You can declare with your mouth, but you must believe it in your heart and your mind. That's where prayer comes in, and we know that prayer changes things, but most importantly, it changes us! So, let's bombard heaven on behalf of our thoughts so we can begin to live a bondage-free life!

LET US PRAY

Heavenly Father, I'm grateful that despite all I've been through, I still have a mind to bless and praise Your name. I ask God that You search my heart and mind and bring any and all thoughts that are contrary to Your Word and who You say I am to the forefront of my mind. I renounce all negative thoughts from the enemy or the inner me. I cancel the spirit of recall and the act of recounting negative situations and events that lead to negative thinking. I decree and declare that I will not allow my past to dictate my thoughts, but I will think on those things that are true, honest, just, pure, lovely, and worthy of praise. All of these things describe You, and because I abide in You, all of these things surround me. Therefore, I thank You – In Jesus' name, amen.

REFLECTION

Take "those things" that Paul mentions we ought to think
on and write what is good about God and what is good
about you (because of God).

GOD	YOU
True	
Honest	
Just	
Pure	
Lovely	
Worthy of Praise	

What you think
determines your
speech
and actions.

God's Timing is Everything

ECCLESIASTES 3:1 (KJV)

*To everything there is a season, and a time to every
purpose under the heaven.*

As we matriculated through school and grew into young adulthood, we started to take thought about where our lives were headed and what we wanted to be and do when we became full-grown adults. Sadly, for many of us (particularly women), our thoughts were more centered around relationship goals than academic or career goals. On the other hand, it could've been a mix of both, with relationship goals being the priority.

Dreams of college degrees followed by a great dating life, courtship, engagement, marriage, and babies... the dream of having a family was and is the ideal. Most women have grown up creating timelines, having a secret savings account for wedding celebrations, putting dreams on hold waiting for a partner- that special person to "do life with."

If I just plan right by this age I'll be... and by this age that'll happen, and by that age I'll have that... You had the perfect timeline and everything under control...

But you're still single.

Or, you got married, and it didn't work out, so now you're single again.

So, where do you go from here?

First, you must understand what season you're in. In the book of Ecclesiastes, the writer Solomon, a man full of wisdom, provides one of the greatest pieces of advice: TIMING IS EVERYTHING. There is a time and a purpose for everything we go through and everything we experience and encounter. The mistake we make is trying to create situations that fit into our time or season instead of positioning ourselves to be ready for THE RIGHT time and season. For example, if you plant a seed in good soil during a time that is not conducive to that seed, it will not yield a harvest. If you plant that same seed during the right time, but the ground hasn't been cultivated to receive that seed, it still will not yield a harvest. The point is, not only do the seed and the soil need to be right, but the timing has to be right also.

There is a reason you are single or single again in this season. It doesn't necessarily mean your seed is bad, and it doesn't necessarily mean the soil is either. The timing may not be right. The only way to know if and when the time is right is to understand what season you're in.

One of the greatest commodities we have is time, and often, as singles, we waste our time chasing the dream of a relationship in the wrong season and miss out on key opportunities to maximize our time alone, which will prepare us for the right season. Do you really know who you are? Do you really know what you want? Do you really know what you *don't* want? Using this season of singleness will help to bring clarity into your life if you allow it.

After my previous relationship went awry, I had pressed the pause button to sort out my life, my past experiences, and my choices in men. I started to seek God and take inventory of the type of men I allowed into my life and why. I then pressed the reset button to bring me back to my original factory settings before all of the hurt, disappointment, betrayal, and foolish decisions ensued. There was a power I attained as a result of taking control of my emotions and giving them to God to sort out and make sense of them for me. This season of singleness has brought the clarity I needed, so when the next season approaches, I will know it and will act accordingly.

What are you doing in your season of singleness? What season are you in? Is this the season to get to know yourself and deal with past hurts? Is this the season to work on your career goals and get your credit in order? Knowing the season you're in will take the edge off the desire to be in a relationship. It will put things in the right perspective and prevent you from looking crazy or being in situations that are no good for you. Being sure of where you are in life will give you peace of mind! It will also protect you from unwanted hurt and disappointment. I encourage you to embrace this season of singleness. Take control of your season and maximize it, so you can position yourself and be prepared for the next one!

LET US PRAY

Father, I come to You with thankfulness and gratitude. I bless Your name because You know where I am in this stage of my life. You are in complete control; help me remember that during this season. I ask God that You reveal to me what this season is about. Show me the purpose of this time and how to use it and maximize it wisely. Show me the things I need to work on and what needs to be worked out of me. Above all, help me to embrace and own the season I am in. Help me to enjoy it unashamedly, with no regrets. Give me the tools I need in this season to prepare and position myself for the next one. In Jesus' name, amen!

REFLECTION

What season of singleness are you in?

_____

_____

_____

_____

_____

_____

How do you plan to use your time during your season of
singleness?

_____

_____

_____

_____

_____

_____

_____

_____

God's timing
is everything

Living Single

Teach me how to live, O Lord. Lead me along the right path, for my enemies are waiting for me.

believe one of the reasons singleness is so frowned upon is because there haven't been real conversations about how to live successfully single. The only topics that are mentioned regarding singleness are sexual impurity, lust, fornication, and how not to fall and fail as an unmarried person. These topics are often glossed over with Scripture, followed by all of the negative consequences of having sex before marriage.

For this reason, people are merely feeling their way through singleness instead of embracing it and failing miserably most times. Singleness is often a matter of trial and error and then being put on trial for your error if and when you are exposed (i.e., pregnant out of wedlock). Advice for singles is reactive rather than proactive, and it is often given by those who are married with the aforementioned counsel of *what not to do,* rather than providing the tools of *how not to do.*

I believe the reason is there are very few married people who lived a single life successfully before getting married themselves. On the contrary, there are people who actually lived and are living a completely pure (virgin) life or a partially pure (celibate) life during their singleness. There are couples who took vows of sexual purity and celibacy before getting married. There are single women and men (I know, shocking) who have dedicated their lives to God and are living successfully single and are happy. Yes, actually happy. Yes, it is quite possible to live a sex-free, happy life.

Anything that God approves of, the enemy disapproves. So, while God makes a way of escape for you so you can live a pure, happy, drama-free life, the enemy desires to do the exact opposite. The enemy will bring people into your life to pose as a potential mate, but they will be the furthest thing from it. You will know this because that counterfeit will set out to undo everything God has done. They will set out to speak against the Word of God and what is right. They will be anti-god, having a form of godliness but denying its power. Note: the plan of the enemy won't always be so subtle.

They might say, "no one is really keeping themselves," or make you feel bad for wanting to save yourself for marriage. This is why it is extremely important to pray to God that He shows you how to live a single successful life. When you've made up in your mind what you will not tolerate, it will be easier to walk away from those who do not share the same morals and values as you. Ask God to show you how to live and to put people in your life who can help navigate you through singleness and provide you with wise counsel. You need strong people who've lived successfully single, and successfully dated without falling into temptation. You even need those who have slipped up and will be truthful about their journey and not act like they lived a perfect single life. God will grant you the desires of your heart if you truly desire it. Now, let us pray!

LET US PRAY

Heavenly Father, I thank You for giving me the desire to live right and to seek You for guidance on how to do so. You are the God of wisdom, so I pray that You impart Your wisdom unto me. Teach me, Lord, how to live right. Teach me, Lord, how to live a successful single life. Continue to give me the desire to want to live right every day. I pray, Lord, for discernment. Show me who is safe and who is a snare. Put divine connections in my life, those who can offer wise counsel and help me along my journey until You see fit to change my status. When it is time for me to date, thank You for placing only those who share the same godly morals and values that I share. I thank You in advance for it, in Jesus' name, amen!

REFLECTION

Thoughts:

Anything that
God approves,
the enemy
disapproves.

Lord, I Trust You!

*Trust in and rely confidently on the Lord with all
your heart and do not rely on your own insight
or understanding. In all your ways know and
acknowledge and recognize Him, And He will make
your paths straight and smooth [removing obstacles
that block your way].*

Our entire walk and belief system is based on faith in God. It's based on the unknown with the understanding and belief that the unknown does exist, and we don't have to tangibly see things to believe they exist. No one has seen God, but we believe that He exists. His Word is real, and His promises are yea and amen.

As human beings, we were born with five senses- sight, touch, smell, taste, and hearing. It is the way we navigate through life and the way we determine how we feel. The issue arises when we rely solely on how we feel and what we see over what God says. It is this issue that trips singles up often. We look at our circumstances and where we are. We use our age, list of goals, where we think we ought to be, and when all of those entities don't add up, we tend to want to take matters into our own hands. That includes trying to look for (or be found by) a suitable partner.

We start to go against our better judgment just to check off our goals list, not knowing that it will only be a matter of time before we realize that we've created new problems that make what we thought the old ones were (being single) a walk in the park. All because we took matters into our own hands and didn't acknowledge God and include Him in our decision making, or take heed to His NO or NOT YET.

My friend, please know you don't have to go through hellfire and then look back in hindsight and have a paper trail of lessons to pass on to someone else. There are enough of us who took matters into our own hands or weren't mature in God to see the pitfalls that have that "had I known then what I know now" testimony. THAT DOESN'T HAVE TO BE YOUR TESTIMONY! If you are single with no children, no issues, and no drama, keep that same energy! Now, if you do have that testimony, or if you're currently knee-deep in mess, you can still ask God to come and straighten it out. He is waiting for you to just speak the word so He can come and help you sort out those pieces and start life afresh. Above all, I pray that you learn to trust God in every situation, no matter how hard things get or how hard things seem.

LET US PRAY

Lord, I declare on today that I trust You. I trust You with my life, my circumstances, my present, and my future. I invite You into every area of my life. I submit my desires to You. I place my dreams and goals at Your feet. Father, I recognize that without You, I can do nothing. Without Your approval and Your leading, I will make a shipwreck of my life. So, I acknowledge You, Lord, in all my ways, and I ask You to come in and remove every roadblock and obstacle in my life, whether it be a person, a place, a thing, or even ME. Remove every hindrance that will prohibit me from walking into my divine destiny. In Jesus' name, I pray, amen.

REFLECTION

What areas of your life have you relinquished and given to God?

_____

_____

_____

_____

_____

_____

_____

What areas of your life are you trusting God with NOW?

_____

_____

_____

_____

_____

_____

_____

_____

Trust God!!!

Goodbye to Guilt and Shame

ROMANS 8:1 (NLT)

So now there is no condemnation for those who belong to Christ Jesus.

One of the biggest challenges I had was fighting against guilt and shame. If I can be honest, I've made some horrible mistakes as a single woman. I've gotten into situations that proved to be demonic sanctions from hell to destroy my destiny. I've accepted toxicity disguised as love, and when the truth was exposed, I made excuses because I didn't know how to get out of what I was in. I compromised my values and the type of love I knew I deserved for what I thought was the only thing I was capable of receiving. With every decision, acceptance, and compromise, every relationship crashed and burned and left me with scars that can't be seen by most.

With every relationship calamity, I repented to God. It seemed like a vicious cycle. The enemy in true fashion worked tirelessly to pile on spirits of heaviness, guilt, and shame. He whispered in my ear the mistakes I've made. The enemy repeated to me the conversations those he hired were having. He did his best to convince me that I would never be forgiven, never be happy, and would never bounce back from all of the heartbreak, mistakes, and foolish decisions I made in my life, but that's not what my Bible says! With every attack, I learned how to counter-attack. I declared who I was based on what the Bible says about me rather than what the enemy was saying about me.

When you honestly repent and seek to learn from your errors, turn away, and be/do better, you gain a power that enables you to speak what the Word says. How? Because you're free! Once you are free, you are able to openly testify where you've been, the mistakes you've made, and how God delivered you. When you're free and gain the courage to tell of God's goodness and mercy, you take the adversary's power away to use your story as a ransom for his ego and your demise.

I dare you to declare that you're taking back your power! I dare you to start looking at the mistakes of your past as the lessons of what not to repeat in your present and future. Because you're in Christ, you cannot be condemned because everything you've done was already nailed to the Cross. When you repent (ask for forgiveness and turn away from the sin you're asking for forgiveness for), the enemy no longer has legal authority over your life or your story. If you are dealing with guilt and shame based on past (or present) decisions, I encourage you to release yourself into the loving, powerful arms of God, allow the healing process to begin, then, once you've been strengthened, help someone else with your story. Let's pray and declare it!

LET US PRAY

Spirit of the True and Living God, I come humbly before You to say thank You! Thank You because You knew me before I was created. You knew every foolish mistake, ill-decision, pitfall, and situation I would end up in. You knew the relationships I would partake in, and You knew the consequences I would have to endure. I am reminded that everything I've gone through, You went through when You hung on the Cross for the remission of my sins! Everything I've done and will do You died for, and it is under Your blood. Therefore, I decree and declare that because I am in You, every single thing I've done is under the footstool of Jesus!

I ask You, God, to clean my heart and renew a right spirit within me. Loose the shackles of oppression. I renounce the spirit of guilt and shame over my life. Because I have confessed my faults, You are able to cleanse me from all unrighteousness and I thank You even now for it being so! I am not condemned, but I am in Christ! In Jesus' name, AMEN!

REFLECTION

Be bold! Write down the things God has delivered you from. Make a mark of it so it can serve as a reminder of your victory!

_____

_____

_____

_____

_____

_____

_____

_____

_____

_____

_____

_____

_____

_____

_____

Guilt and shame
have
no place in your
life!

Uprooting Jealousy

PROVERBS 14:30 (NLT)

*A peaceful heart leads to a healthy body;
jealousy is like cancer in the bones.*

Stress, anxiety, drama… it all can weigh you down mentally, emotionally, and physically. We don't realize it, but our emotions start in our hearts, travel to our minds, and come through our actions. Most times, people do not realize what they are really thinking and how they are really feeling because they are not consciously aware of what they are saying or doing in the heat of the moment. However, if you listen intently to a person speak, if they speak long enough, they will reveal their heart.

The Bible says to guard your heart, for out of it flow the issues of life (Proverbs 4:23). It is important as a single person to constantly keep the lines of communication open with God regarding how you're feeling. It's very easy to get caught up in the desire to be in a relationship because of what society puts before us. This causes us to create unnecessary drama not only for ourselves but for other people.

Being single in and of itself can be tricky. You already have a lot working against you, seemingly happy relationships, engagements and weddings, movies, and TV shows with storylines about love in the media. Add to that the lack of information, wise counsel, and support about being single. The last thing you want to do is add jealousy to the list. No matter how innocent you may think it is, no matter how much sense you think it makes, jealousy is ugly. It's nasty, it's evil, and it's hurtful. It spreads from your heart to your mind, then to your actions and your reactions, and if unchecked, rots you to your core. Above all, jealousy is the antithesis to living an abundant life. Jealousy is counter-productive to the blessings you expect because God is not going to honor anything a jealous person does because their motives are vicious and calculating.

I can't stress enough the importance of living a free life full of peace. Be of good courage! Wait on the Lord and wait for His best for you. I've never met a jealous person who was happy and satisfied with their life. If you've found yourself being jealous of another person, particularly of another's relationship, no judgment! Take your concerns to the Lord and ask Him to clean your heart and remove the bitter, nasty taste of jealousy from your heart. Focus on all of the wonderful things you have going for you, and seek to always be content where you are. God is able to heal, deliver, and set free because God cannot fail! Let's go to the throne of grace!

LET US PRAY

Heavenly Father, I humbly approach Your throne with a repentant heart. God, I ask You to search my heart in the inward parts and show me if there is any jealousy in me towards a person or another's relationship. If there is, I pray that You remove those feelings of jealousy from my heart. I pray that You convict me if and when I desire to say or do anything that could jeopardize another person's relationship. I pray that You convict me if and when I find myself wanting to pray against someone else's happiness. Deliver me from sowing seeds of negativity in another person's life, as the seeds that I sow will be the harvest produced in my life, and I want to sow good seed in good ground in other people as well as myself. May I always remember that what You have for me is for me! What You have for me cannot be taken away, and what is not for me cannot stay; therefore I will not operate in evil trying to ruin someone else's happiness because that is not of You. I thank You, Lord, for peace and true happiness in You.
In Jesus' name, amen!

REFLECTION

Thoughts:

_____

_____

_____

_____

_____

_____

_____

_____

_____

_____

_____

_____

_____

_____

_____

_____

_____

_____

Jealousy is nasty, evil, & hurtful.

DAY 10

Motives are Everything

PHILIPPIANS 2:3-4 NLT

Don't be selfish; don't try to impress others. Be humble, thinking of others as better than yourselves. Don't look out only for your own interests, but take an interest in others, too.

I remember having a conversation with some single women some time ago. At the time, they were single, having never been married, and I was single and divorced. We got into the topic of the infamous lists singles often make (and are encouraged to make) about the type of spouse they desire. These women began their list of things they were *not* going to do first. I sat quietly, listening to their rants as they then began to give me their long laundry list of who they expected their husband to be and what they expected him to have and do. Upon completion of their exhaustive list, I asked them if they had a list of what they were going to bring to the table (contribute to the marriage). They fumbled their words and in response somehow went back to their list of things they were not going to do. The things they did agree to do came with conditions. I listened in horror at the firestorm of potential issues their marriages would have. I even challenged them with scenarios and "what ifs" to see how they would respond to certain situations that could happen in their hypothetical marriage. As we talked, the discussion became heated (playfully) because they were very strong-minded regarding their views and how their marriages would work based on their wants, desires, and demands.

These women are examples of singles who are so caught up in the idea of the engagement, the ring, the ceremony, and the perks of marriage, that they have no clue and, in some cases, want to remain clueless about the ministry of marriage. May I interject here that this is not only an issue with women but with men as well. Yes, there are men who have in their back pocket an exhaustive list of demands of wants, and needs from their future spouse yet, seldom take the time to jot down what they have to offer and bring to the table.

Why is this? In my experience and dealings with singles, it is because a lot of single people desire to get married out of selfish ambition. They want to be able to say that they did it they found a suitable person to recite vows to, and they were able to do like everyone else did, never taking into account the totality and the seriousness of the vows they take BEFORE GOD.

My friend, this is not how things ought to be. Marriage is supposed to be a lifetime commitment. It is a serious ceremony and a serious vow and should not be entered into without clear thought and understanding of what it is you're getting into. As simple as it appears in the media, make no mistake, divorces are just as serious as the vows taken in marriage. Why? Because in marriage, the two become one creating a rebirth of husband and wife, and in divorce the oneness is severed, causing the dissolving and the death of not only the marriage but of the persona of the husband and wife. It's devastating and nothing to be played with. Those reading this book who have suffered and survived divorce understand me clearly. Those who are single and have never been married, trust me, you don't want any parts of a divorce.

So, as we continue on this journey of singleness, if your desire *is* to be married, I challenge you to really think, pray and journal the reasons why you want to get married. I challenge you to not only make your list of what you expect from your future spouse but to also make a list of what you have to offer. Note: the list you make of what you have to bring to the table should be longer than your demands of what you desire from a spouse and deal breakers. Marriage is about the law of reciprocity, and if you don't have anything to offer your future spouse and marriage but have a long list of returns and expectations, your marriage will be one-sided and unfair to the person whom you are marrying, and they don't deserve that!

Remember, our Scripture for today talks about taking an interest in others too. Yeah, THAT PART! Your interest should be so wrapped up in serving the one you want to spend the rest of your life with, that they will desire to return the favor. That is the law of reciprocity! A strong healthy marriage is about two people who live their entire life competing for who can serve the other best. I encourage you to check your motives for wanting to be married and submit your request to the Lord. The right motives will yield the right results.

LET US PRAY

Gracious God, I thank You for being who You are. I thank You for knowing me inside and out. I thank You, God, because only You know my true motives. I want my motives for everything I do to be pure, especially concerning marriage. So, I pray that You show me my true motives for getting married. I pray that You give me the courage to admit to all of my reasons and to correct me regarding the motives that do not line up with Your purpose. I pray, God, that You help me to get rid of any and all selfish motives that serve as reasons I want to be married. Help me to seek the institution of marriage the way You designed it and for the reasons You created it. Help me to create pure motives for marriage. In Jesus' name, I pray, amen!

REFLECTION

Think about the reasons you want to be married
and list 3 below:

_____

_____

_____

_____

This book is for you and about you. Instead of writing your
list of what you desire in a spouse, list the things you
have to bring to the table. What amazing things do you
have to offer your spouse? List ten (YES, ten!).

_____

_____

_____

_____

_____

_____

_____

_____

_____

Why do you want to be married?

Make Peace with Your Past

COLOSSIANS 3:13 (NLT)

Make allowance for each other's faults, and forgive anyone who offends you. Remember, the Lord forgave you, so you must forgive others.

et me hit you with the headliner: you will not have a fulfilling relationship or marriage if you carry unforgiveness in your heart from past hurts.

I already spoke about the wrong motives for wanting to get married, but there is another alarming ill motive that I didn't mention. Some singles want to get married just to prove to those who broke their heart that they are worthy of love and capable of being loved by someone else.

You were always worthy of love darling, that person was just not the one designed to love YOU. I've seen it in my lifetime, women (because this is mostly a women's issue) who are heartbroken and embarrassed that the man they were with broke up with them or didn't see them as marriage material, who rushed to find a man so they could prove to the world they're not who people think they are (undesirable, not worthy of love).

The finding of a new "Boo" is the smokescreen for forgiveness. The new relationship says, "I've moved on, and I have someone who will love me now, so I forgive you." This couldn't be farther from the truth. How can one tell? If the man with who the woman is no longer in a relationship with moves on, that woman will most times throw serious shade not only towards him but his new Boo! This is the tell-tale sign that the ex has not forgiven him and has not moved on, which proves the point that you cannot replace old hurt with new love. You must allow the hurt to heal and true forgiveness to take place before you move into another relationship!

I've seen countless times women who claimed to have moved on in happy relationships but were still shady to their ex. Not every breakup renders a friendship, but all too often, the woman is bitter even while in another relationship. For this reason, it pays to forgive and make peace with your past. Otherwise, you're not looking for a relationship; you're looking for a replacement.

After a very hurtful and very public breakup I endured, the one thing I refused to do was jump back into the dating scene immediately to prove anything to anyone. I must admit, it was very difficult living through mounds and mounds of gossip, lies, laughter, and opinions about how "something had to be wrong with me." I'll say again, singleness is already seen as a prison or a death sentence, especially in the church, so to add on divorce and another engagement and then another one who walked away, SURELY something has to be wrong with me! In most cases, one would try to figure out a way to prove their worth to people just for the sake of clearing their name. However, my healing and getting through the process of forgiveness were more important than proving a point to people.

Today, two years later, I've forgiven every single person who was involved directly or indirectly and was a "stakeholder" in the quest to make sure I didn't receive what they thought would be my "happy ending." I'm stronger, even more solid in who God created me to be, and I am living my life in God and enjoying my season of singleness mostly because I chose to forgive! If I can do it with all I've been through, you can too. Let's pray about it!

LET US PRAY

Father, I come to You on today thanking You for being who You are. I also come today with a repentant heart. I come to repent for holding unforgiveness in my heart towards (name the person or people). I am sorry because I cannot expect You to forgive me for the wrong I've done towards You AND others if I don't forgive those who've done wrong towards me. So, I'm asking that You will blot out that person's transgressions towards me. I'm asking Lord that You have mercy on them for what they've done to me, and I ask You to create in me a clean heart and renew a right spirit within me (Psalm 51:10). God, I want to forgive so I can live freely and prepare myself for my future because I want all that You have for me. Today I evict those people and situations that have been renting space in my head and heart, so I can make space for what and who You have, especially for me. I decree and declare, You have forgiven me, I have forgiven, and I am free.
In Jesus' name, amen!

REFLECTION

Do some self-reflection: is there anyone that you need to forgive? Is there a situation from your past you still need to heal from? Write it down below and make a commitment to start the healing process.

Heal from the hurt before you get into another relationship!

Be Wise!

PROVERBS 4:7 (NLT)

Getting wisdom is the wisest thing you can do! And whatever else you do, develop good judgment.

There are so many positive benefits to being single! Being single in your adulthood is paramount because you get to discover who you are and where you are in your life. One of the biggest weapons a single person can obtain is wisdom. Wisdom is described as the soundness of an action or decision with regard to the application of experience, knowledge, and good judgment.

In this time of singleness, you literally have the world in the palm of your hands. In order to have the world in the palm of your hands, however, you have to put your life in the center of God's will. The center of God's will is where you will find wisdom. The center of God's will is where you find instruction. The center of God's will is where you learn what good judgment is and develop discernment to make the right decisions concerning your life.

Wisdom will show you who to entertain and who to stay away from. Wisdom will cause you to have good judgment in your decisions and have the courage to walk away from a temporary situation that could cause a lifetime of regret, and wait for God's purpose and plan for your life so you can have a lifetime of love and happiness. So today, we're going to bombard heaven and pray for wisdom concerning our life and our singleness. Let's go to the Throne of Grace!

LET US PRAY

Gracious God, our eternal Father, I come today to tell You that I love You! I love You because You have loved me with an everlasting love. Lord, I come today to ask for wisdom and sound judgment. I'm asking You for wisdom concerning my entire life; my finances, my decisions, my job, everything that concerns me. I pray for good judgment when it comes to making decisions regarding who I should entertain. Give me a discerning spirit to see the true heart, motives, and intentions of those I come in contact with. Show me who is not good for my mind, soul, and spirit, and give me the courage to walk away, dismiss, cut off and remove myself from potential toxic relationships AND friendships. I decree and declare that loneliness and desperation WILL NOT be my portion! I will not follow my heart and not think with my head. I will not ignore the red flags and the warning signs You send. I will not dismiss the feelings in the pit of my stomach or the nerves in my body that show as signal danger. I will take heed, allow You to take the lead, use wisdom and sound judgment, and save myself from pain and regret in Jesus' name, AMEN!

REFLECTION

Thoughts:

Wisdom will show you who to entertain and who to stay away from.

Living with the Wounds

2 CORINTHIANS 12:8-9 (NLT)
Three different times I begged the Lord to take it away. Each time he said, "My grace is all you need. My power works best in weakness." So now I am glad to boast about my weaknesses, so that the power of Christ can work through me.

The Apostle Paul in 2 Corinthians 12 is discussing some sort of ailment he had. The Bible doesn't tell us what that ailment was, but Paul describes it as "a thorn in his flesh" (verse 7). A thorn is a sharp, stiff, and rigid projection on a plant. It symbolizes sorrow and hardship. So, we can draw the conclusion that thorns are sharp, they hurt when touched, can be inconvenient l and quite painful if you get poked by one. It's safe to say that whatever Paul's "thorn" was, it was painful and inconvenient; otherwise, he wouldn't have asked God to remove it three times. God never removed the thorn but responded to Paul that his grace (God's) was sufficient, so sufficient that in Paul actually enduring the weakness, God's power was exhibited.

Single life is not always lived under 100% chastity, purity and perfection. All have fallen short, and singles are not exempt. For that reason, it is important to go to God with the truth about our "thorns." Your thorn may be depression because you are single. Another person's thorn may be lusting after another person due to loneliness as a result of singleness. Another person's thorn may be envy over someone else's relationship or marriage due to a breakup that results in them being single again. Someone else's thorn could very well be an addiction to pornography because they have a hard time keeping their flesh under subjection. These are thorns because they hurt us and can prevent us from living our best life.

The mistake we make is covering these thorns and acting like they don't exist for fear of judgment and ridicule. When real conversations about real feelings and real struggles don't happen, bondages are created. Singles are either living secret lives of sin or are so pent up with nowhere to release their true feelings and be free that they become mean and harmful to themselves and those around them. Consider this: those feelings, those thorns as we call them, while they are not good, they are the vices used to remind us that we are human and in need of a Savior who can deliver us! Even if He doesn't deliver, and even if you continue to have those feelings, His strength is made perfect because you are able to own up to your weakness and allow Him to come and be with you in your struggle!

Most of us see singleness as a thorn. Like Paul, looking for God to remove the thorn, but what if we flipped the switch and focused on his grace instead of the "thorn" of singleness?

Singleness seems cute when you are a teenager, but

for some reason, once you hit twenty-five, it seems like the plague. The list of goals comes out, the clock starts ticking, and every day alive is one in which we think we should be in a relationship and on the way to marriage. It's so bad that people who are single make finding (or being found by) a spouse a part of their daily prayers. I've said it before, and it may become a common thread throughout this devotional: singleness is seen as a problem and something to get rid of and out of quickly.

As much as you may despise singleness, it is not a thorn. The things you may go through as a result of singleness may feel like your thorn. I challenge you to go to God honestly and unashamedly and talk to Him about your weaknesses. Give them to God and tell Him how you really feel. Once you do this, watch God sweep through your life with His grace and make living the single life more bearable!

Singleness is not a holding cell in prison where you sit in bondage, waiting to be found by someone to break you out, love you and jump start your life. Singleness is a time to learn all of who you are, see where you need to grow, and work on the things missing in your life so that you can be the best version of yourself for yourself every single day. In doing this, you will be preparing for your spouse as well. Let us go to the throne of grace and lay our weaknesses at His feet so we too can have the testimony that God's grace truly is sufficient, and His strength is being made perfect in our weakness!

LET US PRAY

Abba Father, I come to You today with thankfulness in my heart. Thank You, Lord, for being a God who understands our issues and weaknesses. You were tempted above all yet knew no sin (scripture). You hung on the Cross, bearing every single burden, infirmity, and feeling I would go through. What a wonderful God You are! Who wouldn't serve a God who is full of compassion and empathy towards my feelings! Lord, I come to You with my feelings of

_____,

_____,

_____

and

_____.

I lay every weakness at Your feet. I unashamedly confess with my mouth that I have these situations and feelings, but I have the assurance of knowing that Your grace is sufficient and Your strength is made perfect in my weakness. So today, I trade my weakness for Your strength; I trade my burdens for Your peace, and I trade my feelings for the truth of what You said in Your Word. Until You change the situation, I thank You for changing me in the situation. In Jesus' name, amen!

75

REFLECTION

It's always good to document where you are so you can track your progress and look back later to see how far you've come. Take a moment to write what you've been struggling with as a testimony, believing by faith that God has delivered you and has indeed traded your weakness and given you His strength to endure during this time of singleness.

Singleness is not
a prison sentence.

I Have No Reason to Fear

2 TIMOTHY 1:7 (KJV)
*For God hath not given us the spirit of fear;
but of power, and of love, and of a sound mind.*

One of the fears some single people have is the possibility of being single forever. The fear of being single goes far beyond not having anyone to be in a godly covenant with, where sex is permissible (as opposed to fornication and sexual sin). I want to challenge you to change your mindset and confessions. Instead of confessing FEAR, confess you have CONCERNS.

Make no mistake, the concerns you may have about being single are real and valid. There are concerns about doing life alone, such as the concern of not having someone to plan a future with. You may be concerned about who you will turn to or who will be there for you should you get sick or have some type of emergency. These are real concerns, and no one can tell you not to feel the way you feel (especially if they are married). HOWEVER, the danger comes when your concerns turn into fear.

There is an acronym for fear that I'm sure you've heard. Fear is "False Evidence Appearing Real." Fear, by definition, is an unpleasant emotion caused by the belief that someone or something is likely to cause pain or a threat. So, in essence, fear is the false evidence that causes an unpleasant emotion due to a threat that appears real but may not necessarily be real. What's my point? My point is, it's okay to have honest concerns about your singleness, but don't you dare allow your concerns to turn into fear. Why? Because fear causes you to react to your situation rather than respond. Fear causes you to act on and react to your emotions rather than make sound decisions concerning your life. Fear is NOT of God! Fear comes from hell and is not how we ought to live.

On the contrary, God has given us power, love, and a sound mind. My friend, you have the power of God on your side to overcome the uncomfortable feelings of the unknown future. You have the power to speak the Word of God over your situation and speak to the uneasiness your heart may be feeling about being single. You have the love of God to first show you how much you are loved BY God, which will then cause you to love yourself and understand that this season of singleness is not punishment, but it's preparation for your future. Understanding how much you're loved by God will cause you to love Him all the more, which will give you a sound mind, understanding that where you are is in the center of God's will and He is in control. He knows what's best for you, and because of that, you can rest easy! Now, let us pray!

LET US PRAY

Gracious God, I thank You for this day. I thank You for being God all by yourself. Father, I come to You with the feelings I feel and the concerns I have about being single. God, You know me better than I know myself. You know the things I have not articulated and the deeply rooted concerns I have. I pray against fear right now in the name of Jesus. I decree and declare that fear is not my portion. I reject and renounce fear in my life. I break up with fear in my heart right now. I declare on this day that You, Lord, have endowed me with Your power, Your love, and a sound mind to think right, act right, walk right and talk right. I proclaim that on this day, I am in the center of Your will, and because You are the Author and Finisher of my life, I will not worry, and I will not fear. You are in complete control, and for that, I say, "THANK YOU!"

REFLECTION

Thoughts:

_____

_____

_____

_____

_____

_____

_____

_____

_____

_____

_____

_____

_____

_____

_____

_____

I have no
reason to fear!

Stay Focused!

PROVERBS 4:27 (NLT)
Don't get sidetracked;
keep your feet from following evil.

t's easy to look around you and get sidetracked. It's easy to fall into the rabbit hole of loneliness, especially when you see others in relationships. There will be some seasons where it's quiet. There won't be much talk about relationships in your circles of influence or on social media. Then all of a sudden, BOOM! Everywhere you look, folks are in love, getting engaged, and flooding your timeline with wedding plans and marriage photos.

Here's the thing: it is very possible to see all of the news of new relationships, engagements, and marriages on your timeline and around you, be happy for them, and not fall into a state of depression. As I write this devotional, I remember going through a season in my healing process from a really public and really devastating breakup, where there were four engagements at my church in a three to six-month period. Everywhere I turned around, someone was showing up with a ring on her finger. I learned (and even witnessed some) of these engagements close to the year following what was supposed to be my wedding date. Fast forward a year later, one of my very best friends got engaged in June, and in July, the very same month I was supposed to get married three out of the four couples that got engaged, got married!

I could've easily gotten sidetracked. I could've easily fallen hard into depression, recounting what was supposed to be in my own life. I could've recalled and rehearsed all of the hurt and pain I endured, sulking about my own life instead of celebrating the happiness of others. I could've allowed my feet to slip by going back to my vomit and entertaining past relationships or trying to find a suitable partner to be with to soothe my feelings. However, I remained focused. How do you remain focused when you're watching everyone else be happy? I'm so glad you asked.

BE HAPPY FOR YOURSELF! Be happy about all of the things you've accomplished. Be happy about where you are in *your* life. Above all, understand the purpose of seasons and the fact that your season has nothing to do with someone else's. Those who got married and are getting married- this is their season. It's not yours (yet). This is their time to shine, to be happy, to celebrate love, and be celebrated by those who are genuinely happy for them, and that should include you! Whatever you do, don't allow your feet to slip and follow evil. For every happy person, there's at least one person who is not, who is waiting to speak against another's happiness. You don't want to be that person nor associate yourself with those types of people. Don't get sidetracked! Congratulate, be happy for others, and stay focused on **your life!**

LET US PRAY

Spirit of the living God, I thank You on today. I thank You for being a real, tangible God. I thank You for Your Word, for it is the guidebook on how to live this life. I pray today for focus. I pray as I journey through my singleness, I don't become consumed by other people's happiness and relationship accomplishments. I pray that I keep myself and my happiness a top priority. Give me the strength to celebrate others without confusing their season with mine. Cause me to be genuinely happy for those who've found love and not slip into evil thoughts, words, or deeds towards those who are happy. I make the declaration that I will not allow someone else's happiness to get me sidetracked. I will stay focused on where I am, how I can be the best version of myself and look forward to what You have for me. In Jesus' name, amen!

REFLECTION

Make a list of the things you're focusing on. Be deliberate

about any projects or goals you want to accomplish.

Stay focused!

God Knows What He's Doing!

JEREMIAH 29:11 (NLT)

*For I know the plans I have for you,' says the Lord.
They are plans for good and not for disaster, to give
you a future and a hope.*

I remember going through a really tough time during my divorce and not understanding what was happening. I couldn't see the end of the suffering, and because my relationship with God was still fresh, I thought that He was just as caught off guard and confused as I was. I thought that because I was "walking with God," we were walking together like two blind people trying to find their way. Clearly, I was wrong!

My friend, I really want you to grab hold of this. When I caught this revelation, it shifted my whole thought process about my life and who God is. For some, this may not be anything new, and for others, it may be mind-blowing. One thing I know for sure: when life flips upside down, it's the one thing that will settle you if you allow it to. This is what I want you to grab hold of:

Nothing catches God by surprise. NOTHING.

God, in His sovereignty, strategically planned out your life before you were even a thought. He carved out the blueprint of your life, planning your destiny and the journey you would take to get there. Not only did He map out the blueprint of your life, but He made allowance for every detour and setback you would face during your journey. God knew every decision you would make before you made it. He knew the path you would take before you took it. He knew the relationships you would get into, the "entanglements" you would get caught up in, and the toxic people you would allow into your life. Those may have been your plans, your mistakes, and your mishaps... they may have been the devil's plans, plots, and schemes, but they were not the plan of God.

You may be sitting right now, thinking about the sum total of your life, your decisions, and where you are right now. Whether you're single or single again, wherever you are in life, you have to know that while you may be unsure of your future, God knows exactly what He's doing! We know that God is a good God. He is a good Father, and He gives good gifts. God doesn't give you toxic relationships or people who will play with your heart and hurt you. Those things come from the enemy to cause you to make bad decisions, lose hope and ultimately abort your purpose.

Once you realize that God knows the thoughts and plans He has for you and you surrender all control of your life to Him, a feeling of peace will come over you. Why? Because He has already told you what His plans are for you! Have you ever had a conversation with a potential love interest or have been in a relationship with someone and asked them, "So where do you see us going?" Or, "What kind of future do you see for us?" and they have no answer? Well, unlike those indecisive people you've dealt with, God has a marvelous plan for your life! What are those plans?

- Those plans are good
- Those plans are prosperous
- They are plans filled with hope and a future

No matter where you are today, no matter what you've been through, and no matter the level of heartache and heartbreak you've endured and have overcome, I challenge you to trust the plan of God for your life. I challenge you to believe with all of your heart that while you don't know all of the details of your future, you can trust the One who does! God knows exactly what He's doing, what He has in store for you, and the manner in which you will receive it. God knows what He's doing! Let us pray!

LET US PRAY

Heavenly Father, I come to You today to say thank You. I thank You for being God above all and the Creator of everything. God, I confess that I haven't always trusted in Your plans for my life. Sometimes I may have gone before You and tried to "help You out," or I disregarded Your plans altogether because I didn't feel like they fit within the confines of my own plans or timeline. So today, God, I repent for not trusting You. I repent for going before You. I repent for thinking that my plans could be better than what You had/have in store for me. I decree and declare that today starts a clean slate. By Your grace, I will no longer succumb to my fleshly desires nor the lies of the enemy. I will wait patiently for You to move on my behalf. I believe that because You are not a man that You should lie nor the son of man that You should repent, You have my best interest at heart. Therefore, as of today, I release and dismiss all of my plans, and I submit my entire life to the counsel of Your will.
In Jesus' matchless name, AMEN!

REFLECTION

Often, writing things down on paper proves to create a greater sense of commitment. List the plans that you previously had before you read this chapter and prayed this prayer as a declaration that you are submitting your life to the will that God has for your life!

_____

_____

_____

_____

_____

_____

_____

_____

_____

_____

_____

_____

_____

_____

_____

_____

_____

Nothing catches God by surprise.

One Day at a Time

So don't worry about tomorrow,
for tomorrow will bring its own worries.
Today's trouble is enough for today.

Time is our greatest commodity, but it can also be our greatest stronghold. When wasted, there is much regret, yet we try to rush time along to fit into our time frame on how we think things ought to be.

If you declared you are submitting your life to the counsel of the will of God but are still worried about your future, I'M COMING FOR YOU. Why? Because I understand how hard it can be. I understand the nagging ticking of a time clock and the fact that time waits for no one. I understand the mind games, where one minute you're believing and trusting God, and the next minute you're in a ball of emotions because you just don't understand what is happening or why nothing is happening. Time is brutal when we feel like we're against the clock, and worrying brings on so many other issues, such as fear and anxiety. The worst thing you can do is be fearful and develop anxiety about something that hasn't happened yet and most importantly, things you can't control.

Now, I'm not talking about being carefree and not planning for a future. There's nothing wrong with goal setting and financial planning and things of that sort, and in fact, it is suggested and welcomed. I'm talking about trying to think yourself into the next six months or the next year or the next decade:

Will I ever meet that special someone? Where will I meet him? When will I find her? What will I be wearing? Will it last? Will this next person be the one, or will it be another lesson for me to learn? Where will we live? What about children? What if he/she's out of state and one of us has to relocate? What if? What if? What if?

STOP.

Planning for tomorrow is time well spent. Worrying about tomorrow is time well wasted. Trying to figure out the future is mentally exhausting. Don't waste your time worrying about something that is out of your control. Focus on what you can control and leave the rest up to God. Everything will happen and will be beautiful in its time when it's supposed to be. Let's go to the throne of Grace and lay our worries at the feet of Jesus.

LET US PRAY

Gracious and eternal God, Creator of time and Ruler of destiny, I come to say thank You for being all of these things and so much more. In fact, You are everything. There is no time or turn of events in my life that You haven't either ordained or allowed to take place for my growth and Your glory. I AGAIN submit every plan to You, or the plans that I was reluctant to trust into Your hands in days past.

I decree and declare that I will not worry about tomorrow, or next week, or next month, or next year. I will stay laser-focused on TODAY and allow You to take care of the rest.

In Jesus' name, amen.

REFLECTION

Thoughts:

_____

_____

_____

_____

_____

_____

_____

_____

_____

_____

_____

_____

_____

_____

_____

_____

_____

_____

Planning for tomorrow is time well spent. Worrying about tomorrow is time well wasted.

Mind Your Emotions

GALATIANS 6:4 (AMP)

*But each one must carefully scrutinize his own
work [examine his actions, attitudes, and behavior],
and then he can have the personal satisfaction and
inner joy of doing something commendable without
comparing himself to another.*

Comparison is the killer of joy. We make the grave
mistake of comparing ourselves to others in so
many ways, including relationships. I remember
having a conversation with someone about singleness and
relationships. She confessed to me that she would sometimes
look at a couple and wonder to herself why the guy chose
the woman he was with or how a particular woman was able
to get with the man she was with. She said she would think
to herself that the guy would probably cheat on the girl (if the
girl wasn't attractive by her standards).

I listened to her in amazement, not understanding how
one would have so much time on their hands to think like
that. Why would someone think that anyway? What kind of
person wishes, hopes, or thinks that a guy would cheat on

the woman he's with?

Sadly, those are the thoughts some singles have. These thoughts come from a deep-seated place of unhappiness and discontentment about their singleness. It's a horrible place to be in because it wastes so much energy on the wrong thing, and it blocks one from actually being found by or attracting who God has for them.

A deeper problem develops during the seasons of marriage proposals and engagements. It's okay if it's one person, but there are seasons where everywhere you turn, someone is posting on social media about their wonderful proposal and engagement. If you're not careful and rooted in your relationship with God, it will cause you to ask questions like how could they find someone, and I can't? What is it about me that I keep going in circles and getting linked up in dead-end relationships while they post on social media gushing with joy and excitement, yet I'm still alone?

This is the worst thing you can do. Comparing someone's life to yours is emotionally and mentally draining. The best thing to do is to not compare what someone else has to what you don't. Be genuinely happy for someone else's happiness without spiraling down into a state of depression, anger, and jealousy.

Take the time to seek God, especially during those seasons where it seems like everyone is in a happy relationship, getting engaged, or getting married while you are still single. Talk to God and tell Him exactly how you feel (He already knows anyway. He's just waiting for you to confess so He can help!). Let us pray!

LET US PRAY

Heavenly Father, I come to You on today on behalf of myself. I haven't come to talk about what is happening in another person's life, what they have, who they're with, or what they have going on. I'm here for myself. Lord, on today, I submit all of my emotions to You. I don't look to the right or the left, but I look to You, who is the Author and Finisher, the Creator and the Source of my faith and my very life. Father, I repent for all of the times I compared my life to someone else's. I repent for all the times I looked at someone else's blessings and compared them to mine. Today, I submit my heart and emotions at Your feet for You to do with them what You wish. I decree and declare today that what You God have for me is for me. So, I submit to the counsel of Your will and will wait and be of good courage for what I've prayed for. While I wait, I will thank You for what You've done for me already. In Jesus' name, amen!

REFLECTION

What emotions have you given to God?

_____

_____

_____

_____

_____

_____

_____

_____

_____

_____

_____

_____

_____

Mind your emotions!

Release & Recover!

EPHESIANS 4:31-32 (NLT)

Get rid of all bitterness, rage, anger, harsh words, and slander, as well as all types of evil behavior. Instead, be kind to each other, tenderhearted, forgiving one another, just as God through Christ has forgiven you.

t's one thing to be single, but it's another thing to be single again. It's one thing to have lived and loved unscathed (meaning without too much hurt), and it's an entirely different thing to barely make it out of a relationship with a piece of your mind and heart.

I remember going through a really, really bad breakup. Before that breakup, I got to see instances where there were women who acted completely out of character. I've seen the absolute ugliness in character from women, from being bitter about not being chosen by a man to the slandering of a man's character and with the woman he did choose. I've seen women actually leave ministries because they just couldn't take seeing the man they were with being in a relationship with another woman. I've heard of women threatening a man if he brought another woman to the church they attended, or even so much as dated another woman in their church. All of these examples were not from a marriage standpoint or even an engagement. If these were the reactions from a relationship, can you imagine how it would feel in a marriage?

Marriage is a covenant, and when the covenant is broken, there is a severing. That severing literally feels like a cut that takes place that separates two entities. It's like a limb being amputated from the body with no anesthesia. Whenever something is severed on the body, bleeding takes place. So, in essence, when we are severed from relationships and marriages, the pain we endure causes us to bleed out on people because we are hurting.

My breakup was very hurtful, very traumatic, and very public. It was such a deep-seated cut that I wasn't sure I would recover from. I dealt with trauma and abandonment before, but I was able to control how much people knew and when (to a certain extent). This time, I felt like I was pinned down, beaten down, robbed of my clothes, and then left in the middle of the street naked and bleeding for everyone to see. To add insult to injury, there were so many people who laughed, jeered, and celebrated what looked like my downfall. There were so many who really believed that God had answered their prayers that I deserved what I got and thought (and even hoped) that I wouldn't recover from the calamity. How could someone stand back up and put one foot in front of the other after being knocked down and dragged? Would I have been so wrong for getting into my feelings, clapping back, cussing them out, and going off? Just one time? The answer is, YES.

I'm sure there's at least one person who will pick up this book who's been through a tumultuous relationship or marriage. You've been through a nasty divorce where way too many people were involved. People slandered your name, provided their opinion (that you didn't ask for) concerning your marriage and why it ended. They discussed your situation at parties, dinners, getaways, and DM chats and text threads.

With all of this, YOU must get rid of all the things that will taint your spirit and especially your heart. Of course, it's hard, and it's not fair. Of course, it hurts to be quiet while others keep doing what they do. Of course, you want to tell your side, lash out and maybe even retaliate. However, YOU CAN'T.

I needed to dedicate this day to the single again, the one who is journeying through the hurt, pain, and devastation of betrayal, divorce, and all of the negative things that come along with it. I want you to know that YOU CAN RECOVER. You can forgive all of those who mistreated, mishandled, misunderstood, misguided, used, abused, left you uncovered, and betrayed you. How do I know? Because I did it. How did I do it? I relinquished and released all of me. I let go of my idea of how people were supposed to pay for what they did and said to me. I laid my thoughts of revenge at the feet of Jesus and allowed Him to be in control of how He would work things out and how He would deal with those who hurt me. I couldn't reduce myself to the level of those who were already beneath me because God would not smile down on me, even if I thought I was justified in whatever negative actions I took.

God did it for me, and He can and will do it for you if you allow Him to. The anguish and pain of heartbreak are devastating, and though many don't take the time to consider the feelings of one who is single again, I want to let you know that I do. I see your hurt, and I feel your pain. I understand the sleepless nights, the heart palpitations, and the tears that no one else sees but you and God. I feel all of that, and I also know that we serve a God who is able to wipe that all away, create in you a clean heart, renew a right spirit in you and heal you from the inside out in such a way that He would have to reintroduce you to yourself. It is only then, once you have learned who you are and embraced the new you, that you will be equipped to be introduced to someone else. So, until that time, work to get rid of all the things that would hold you back, then lean in and embrace God's way of handling your situation. You will be the better for it, trust me. Better yet, TRUST GOD! Let's go to the throne of grace!

LET US PRAY

Dear God,

I confess to You today that I am hurting. I am hurt by the pain of my past. I'm hurt at the rejection I have endured or am enduring. I am disappointed in those who promised to cherish, cover me, and protect my heart. I am embarrassed about the public ridicule and scrutiny I have been or am undergoing.

Today, I take all of my hurts and disappointments, and I lay them all at Your feet. I relieve myself of the negative thoughts that can produce bitterness and anger. I reject the voices of the enemy and of people who speak ill of my situation, my past, and my future. I decree and declare that I am not my past, I am not a failure, and I will recover from this! Heartbreak can't hold me, divorce won't defeat me, and singleness won't stagnate me. No matter what it looks like, I am in the palm of Your hand, God, and as long as I'm in YOUR will, everything is going to be all right. I WILL RECOVER from this and come out better than I was before what happened in my life transpired. I claim it, I believe it, and I receive it. In Jesus' name, amen.

SINGLE-ISH

REFLECTION

Thoughts:

Release
&
Recover

Uprooting Jealousy

JAMES 3:16 (NLT)
For wherever there is jealousy and selfish ambition,
there you will find disorder and evil of every kind.

Jealousy is an ugly character trait that warps the vision of the person who is stricken by it. It is mean, can be surly, blocks vision for the future, and tells lies. Jealousy says that the person you are jealous of is better than you, more deserving than you, and is more blessed than you. Jealousy says a person found by the one is highly favored by God, and because you haven't been found by your person, God doesn't favor you.

Jealousy breeds comparison and hate and can result in murder. Extreme cases can be physical murder, but in this case, I'm speaking about murder in the sense of attempting to kill someone else's happiness because it isn't yours. To take it a step further, jealousy not only causes a person to kill someone else's happiness, but it robs you of your own. I'm aware we tackled jealousy some days ago, but it was important to have it mentioned multiple times in this book. We've talked about how it affects the people who are attacked by those who are jealous of them, but today I want to tackle how jealousy affects the person who carries its weight.

Jealousy will cause you to create scenarios in your head about someone else's life. A social media post, a photo, or seeing live interaction can cause a person to start imagining what another's life is like behind closed doors. Before you know it, you go from imagining the happiness they're displaying publicly to hoping and wishing them harm privately. The aforementioned thoughts described start to swirl in your head, and now you've become consumed with another person's happiness. In doing this, you waste precious time because the more time you spend worrying about and following what someone else is doing, the less time you have to create and build your own happiness.

It becomes very tricky, especially for those who have suffered divorce. The mere appearance of another couple can be a trigger and send you into a whirlwind of sadness and other emotions, and these emotions can subtly cause you to slip into jealousy. It's vital to your emotional intelligence to be honest with triggers, symptoms, and feelings of jealousy when they appear. It is the devil's job to make you feel ashamed about your feelings and keep them to yourself, but please know you don't have anything to be ashamed of. This is how bondage takes root and strongholds are formed, but the Bible says we overcome by the blood of the Lamb and the word of our testimony (Revelation 12:11).

My friend, it is my hope that you don't allow another person's happiness and what they display to the public to become a snare to you. God has so much in store for you, and things may look empty now, but you don't know what's on the horizon. You want to take this time out now to pray, prepare and position yourself for what God has for you, and you can't do that if you're consumed by someone else's life and relationship. My prayer for you on this day is that you will adjust your focus and set your affection on God, who He says you are, and the plans He has for you. My prayer is for you to become so consumed with your life that you get excited about your present and your future and actually start looking forward to the great and amazing things God has in store for you. Now, let us pray!

LET US PRAY

*Heavenly Father, I come to You asking for You to
search my heart. You know me from the inside out,
and You know me better than I know myself. Lord, I
pray that You search me and bring to my attention
any ounce of jealousy I may have towards a person
for whatever reason (relationship, career, ministry,
etc.). Lord, I'm not coming to You this time about
how jealousy will affect them; I'm coming to You
about how jealousy will affect me. I want to be laser-
focused on You. I desire a relationship with You
that is so intense that what is happening in another
person's life does not phase me. I don't want to be
swept away by selfish ambition and all types of
evil at the hands of jealousy because I understand
I'll block all that You have for me if I partake in
such evil. So, I pray for laser focus on MY life, MY
present, MY future, and MY destiny. I purpose in my
heart to pray, prepare and position myself to receive
the blessing You have for me, and I thank You in
advance for the release of those blessings. In Jesus'
name, amen!*

REFLECTION

Thoughts:

Jealousy breeds comparison and hate, and can result in murder.

God's Got It!

Do not be anxious about anything, but in every situation, by prayer and petition, with thanksgiving, present your requests to God. And the peace of God, which transcends all understanding, will guard your hearts and your minds in Christ Jesus.

Anxiety is a feeling of uneasiness about something when you're unsure of the outcome. It is the racing of the heart, sweating of the palms, and heavy breathing. In full throttle, anxiety can bring about light-headedness, heart palpitations, nausea, and panic attacks. Worry, apprehension, agitation, nervousness, stress, and trepidation are the effects of anxiety. Clearly, none of this is of God nor His will for your life.

My amazing single soldier, we don't know what the future holds, but we do know Who holds the future. We don't know when, how, where, or why, but what we do know we serve a God who has all of the answers to our questions. Some questions may be answered immediately; other questions, we'll have to discover the answers to as we journey along in this life.

The worst thing you can do is riddle yourself with worry

about the unknown. Playing scenarios in your head in order to try to figure out what's to come is not going to help. You have to cast all of your cares, concerns, thoughts, and worries at the feet of Jesus. The Word says to not be anxious about *anything*. That means no matter how things look, do not worry. Instead of worrying, pray; make your appeal, and thank God in advance for what's to come. The blessing is in thanking God for what's to come, although you're not sure of the future, being sure that the God of the future will give you a peace that far exceeds any scenario you could imagine regarding how your life is going to turn out. Trust God, trust the plan He has for your life, and trust that He will guard your heart and cover your mind as you wait for your amazing future to unfold.

LET US PRAY

Sweet Lord, I come to You carrying every worry, every concern, every care, every question, every thought, and all anxiety concerning my future to You. I submit my dreams, my hopes, and my desires to You. I want to be in Your will, and I want my dreams to match up with the destiny You created for me before the foundation of the world. I believe that You have my best interest at heart, and whatever the plan is You have for my life, it is going to be unlike anything I could've ever imagined. I thank You for the plan You have mapped out for my life, and I decree and declare today that I trust Your planning and Your timing. I thank You in advance for guarding my heart and covering my mind with Your precious blood that I may rest in You as I await the manifestation of my prayers according to Your will. In Jesus' name, amen.

REFLECTION

What areas in your life have you been anxious about? What thoughts and feelings have you given to God? List those things you have been anxious about as a testament to your faith to relinquish everything to the Lord.

Cheers to an
amazing future!

Inhale Hope, Exhale Doubt!

PSALM 94:19 (NLT)

When doubts filled my mind, your comfort gave me renewed hope and cheer.

Doubt tells us that what we're believing God for won't happen. Doubt is a seed, and once we allow that seed to be planted in our minds, it takes root rather quickly. It's easy for a single person to have doubt settle into their mind. If they're single again, the chances are even greater. In this day and age, it seems as if the dating pool is shallow and full of trash. Everyone is playing games, and relationships and marriages are not lasting. If things look dismal out in the world, then what chance have we? Especially in the *church?* What will come of our love life or chance for marriage? If it were up to us, we would have what we wanted. However, the thing about waiting on that God-ordained relationship is there are many areas that must align before that relationship can materialize. For one, we ourselves have to be ready for a relationship (remember the 3 P's – pray, prepare, and position). Secondly, our person has to be ready and prepared to receive or be received by us. Thirdly, the season has to be right.

Sometimes, we allow external circumstances to dictate our mood and subsequently our moves. We want to get ahead of the doubt so we start to take matters into our own hands. This is the worst thing we can do, because if one of the three areas is not aligned, instead of walking into destiny, we'll be walking into a disaster.

Ask me how I know...

I'm so glad you asked.

I was dating someone, and I received a word that I was going to get married. I was told of the amazing person this man of God would be. The description of who he would be was wonderful, but the problem was (if I could be brutally honest), I didn't take that prophetic word to God to see if what He said lined up with my current dating situation. Needless to say, that word wasn't aligned with that relationship. It would be some months before things would go awry, and I would be left picking up the pieces of my shattered heart and doing it publicly at that.

That last relationship brought back all of the feelings of every relationship I had found myself in and the subsequent failures that always seemed to follow me. It was enough to cause me to take every brick thrown at me by ex-boyfriends and the people who stood by watching and hoping for my demise and create not a wall but a fortress where no one could get in, and I wouldn't dare let myself out. Finally, the doubt set in, to the point where instead of throwing myself out there to try to snag some type of man (which is what women often do after a bad breakup), I secluded myself and shut everyone out.

As time progressed, that same word I received seemed to

revisit me through different people. It was as if it was chasing me, but I was running from it. I didn't want to hear it because it hurt to hope, especially doubting for so long and settling into that place of doubt and unbelief. At some point, I started realizing that the failure of a thing didn't negate the truth of God's promise. God's word is not null and void because things were out of sync. The things that would bring God's word to pass were not in alignment. They weren't even present at that time.

Now, when doubt tries to creep up, I go straight to God. I charge my atmosphere and shift my thinking and environment by audibly reminding everyone of what God said (and by everyone, I mean God and myself). When I start to recount the promises of God over my life, He truly swoops in like the amazing God He is and gives me hope and joy. This hope and joy that is under girded by such love, gives me the courage to think differently and the strength to push doubt to the side and take God at His word.

My friend, don't let what you see make you forget what God said! Don't let what you see make you forget what you've prayed for and are believing God for according to His will! When doubt tries to creep in, don't allow what you see to cause you to go before God or to be ensnared by the tricks of the enemy. Stand fast, stand firm, inhale hope and exhale doubt!

LET US PRAY

Heavenly Father, I come to You today with a confession. I confess that there have been times throughout my life where I have doubted You, Your word, and/or Your plan for my life. I have doubted that what You said would come to pass. I have doubted that I was even deserving of the blessings You've spoken over my life. I that You would build me up in my most holy faith. I pray on today that doubt would not cause me to be ensnared by the enemy or the "inner me" by unfulfilling relationships. I want to be in the center of Your will, God, and I will continue to exercise my faith and wait with hope, and joy, for Your promises because Your promises are yea and amen!

REFLECTION

Have you received a prophetic word concerning a relationship that hasn't come to pass yet? If so, write it below:

_____

_____

_____

_____

_____

_____

_____

_____

_____

_____

_____

_____

_____

_____

_____

_____

_____

_____

_____

Inhale hope,
exhale doubt!

Stay Strong!

Be on guard. Stand firm in the faith.
Be courageous. Be strong.

In the Apostle Paul's letter to the church at Corinth, he gave them practical tools to use as they awaited his next visit. The Corinthian church dealt with a lot of disorder and divisiveness, so Paul provided them with four key instructions on how to live what they believed. Paul's instructions to the church at Corinth were to:

Be on guard against spiritually evil traps and dangers
Stand firm in the faith of what they believed
Behave courageously
Be strong

They say the mind is the devil's playground, and I couldn't agree more. Just as the Corinthian church did, we deal with divisiveness and disorder, but in our minds. The scenarios we create in our heads of past situations we wish we would've handled differently; the relationships we entertained that shouldn't have happened; the things we should've said to that ex before we stopped speaking; the foolishness we tolerated that landed us in unfortunate situations. All of these things play on our mind, and when we're not careful, we start to dwell too long on the past. The next thing you know, you're beating yourself up with regret for the things you allowed into your life.

For the person who has gone through a divorce (I refuse to label anyone as a "divorcee"), the thoughts are far more damaging. Broken covenants, unfulfilled vows, and the severing and death of a marriage will send anyone spiraling into a mental boxing ring. Add on the lack of closure, the chances of seeing your ex-spouse (especially when children are involved), and the exhaustive list of situations that come up when you are divorced, and you have an even greater breeding ground of revisiting the past and thoughts of regret that lead you spiraling down this rabbit hole of despair.

So, what do we do about this? How do we shield and protect ourselves from the fear of the future because of the pain of our past? Let's use the four tools the Apostle Paul advised.

Be on guard against spiritually evil traps and dangers

One of the key evil traps and dangers to be on guard against is triggers. In mental health, a trigger is a flashback of something that transpired in the past. It is a reminder of a past traumatic experience and can result in an overwhelming flow of emotions, including sadness, anger, anxiety, and/or panic. Triggers come in many forms: a song, a phrase, or just the sight of the person you were once in a relationship with. It's important to deal with your past hurts so you'll be able to identify your triggers. This way, they won't appear and catch you off guard, and even if they do, you'll be prepared spiritually to fight AND conquer them.

Stand firm in the faith of what YOU believe

What is your confession as a single or single-again individual? Do you believe you are alone or lonely or do you believe you are all-one (complete and whole, lacking nothing)? Do you believe God has the power to heal you from *all* of your past hurts and traumas? Do you believe you are not a victim nor a prisoner to your past, including your mistakes? Do you believe God has forgiven you for the mistakes of your past? *Have you forgiven yourself?* My friend, **you** decide today what you believe, and once you grab hold of the positive confessions concerning your life, stand firm on what you believe! Now, know you can only stand firm if you stand on something firm. That on which you stand has to be a sound, firm foundation, and that is the Word of God. Standing on God's Word provides a strong, steady foundation where you can plant your feet firmly and take your position where you are today, so you can plan for tomorrow!

Behave courageously

How will you behave based on what you believe? Will you operate in fear, or will you behave like one who has been freed and delivered?

Here's the caveat: you may not feel like you've been delivered some days. Depending on the depth of your past situation, fear may try to creep up and cause you to think that with all you've been through, you have a right to be fearful. With your track record, you'll always be alone. Because of the mistakes you've made, no one will ever love you. Some days, you may wake up and just not feel like being courageous, but you must be ANYWAY.

Take the trip. Go out to eat. Buy the shoes. Write the book. Go out on a date. Accept the compliment. Learn to receive love. Allow yourself to be pursued. Behave with courage because **you believe** you deserve the best!

Be strong

Be confident in who you are, what you survived, and who holds your future. Be relentless in taking control of your life, your thoughts, your beliefs, and your behaviors. Be intentional about what you want out of life from this point forward, then work towards it. Be strong in your faith, knowing that God will perfect everything that concerns you! (Psalm 138:8).

Declaration: I have nothing to fear!

I've mentioned before that the acronym for fear is "False Evidence Appearing Real." The purpose of fear is to cause you to succumb to what you see instead of rising to it. Fear says you can't, but faith says you can. Fear says you won't, but faith says you will. Your past is behind you, and your future is ahead of you. Now, let's take these tools and let us bombard heaven!

LET US PRAY

Gracious God, I come to You today to decree and declare that I have nothing to fear! The past is the past, and I take the lessons I've learned, and I apply them to my life so I can be the best version of myself in my present and future. Lord, help me to apply the four principles Paul gave to the church at Corinth.

Give me and increase my discernment, that I may see any spiritual traps and dangers set up to ensnare me. Help me to stand confidently, believing that the worst is behind me and the very best is ahead of me. Give me the fortitude to live courageously without fear of the future, knowing that You know my ending from my beginning, and I'm in the palm of Your hands.

Lastly, help me to stand strong, especially during those days when I feel weak. Lift me above what I see with my eyes, that I will not allow what I see to cause me to forget what You said in Your Word.

In Jesus' name, amen!

REFLECTION

Write an encouraging letter to yourself using the tools
discussed in this chapter.

_____

_____

_____

_____

_____

_____

_____

_____

_____

_____

_____

_____

_____

_____

Stay strong!

Your Tears Mean Something!

They that sow in tears shall reap in joy.

Being single sometimes hurts. Being single again brings on a different type of hurt. I've highlighted the triggers, people, situations, and circumstances that can cause our tears, but I haven't tackled the actual purpose of our tears.

Often, crying is seen as a sign of weakness. Our men (especially Black men) are told not to cry because "big boys don't cry." Women will hold their tears in, to not show signs of emotion as well. Perhaps, women hold their tears back after a season of crying because they're tired of crying. They may have been asked why they're still crying over the same thing. They may have been told to stop crying because it shows signs of weakness. Some may have been told what I was once told: "Don't let the enemy see you sweat." For all of these reasons, many choose to stop allowing their tears to flow.

I remember hearing that someone I once considered a friend thought of me as a cry baby. I could see that because

I went through a ten-year stint of what seemed like back-to-back hurt, betrayal, and other misfortunes. It seemed like every Sunday; you could find me somewhere in church crying out to God in sheer anguish sometimes. It looked like my life depended on it, and it did. What this girl didn't understand was that while I may have been a nuisance to her, crying was my lifeline. Crying was my non-verbal expression of what I was feeling. When I had no more words, I cried.

I want to dispel the ignorant belief that crying is a sign of weakness. In fact, scientists have discovered that crying could be a way of relieving stress, as traces of stress chemicals were found in tears. Also, some studies suggest that crying causes the body to produce endorphins, which are feel-good chemicals produced by the brain. Ever had one good ole, ugly cry and felt better afterward? No wonder why! You relieved the stress you were carrying!

Psalm 126 was possibly written to celebrate Judah's return from Babylonian captivity (Ezra 1). It speaks to God's ability to restore life into any dead situation, to bring the good out of tragedy and trauma, and even free the oppressed and those in captivity. Verse 5 in this chapter speaks directly to the tears of those who suffered from the grief of loss and calamity as a result of being in captivity. It is the declaration that one day the crying will cease, and you will find joy again in life. There will be a day where you go from grieving the loss of a relationship or lamenting the lack of one to celebrating your strength and fortitude to be an overcomer and find happiness even in the absence of companionship.

So, my friend, don't allow the cares of life and how you're feeling to stress you out! Release your cares and worries, and if you need to cry, CRY! Crying is a human function, and it is healing. God will not allow a single tear to be wasted. He will not allow any tear to fall to the ground without allowing it to become the seed that will produce your harvest. I encourage you when you talk to God, pray, have a bad day, are confronted with a trigger, if you need to cry, let the tears fall! There's no shame in crying. There's no weakness in crying. There is a plan and a purpose for crying, and that purpose includes men as well!

Brother, don't you dare allow ANYONE to tell you you're less of a man for crying and releasing your emotions. You are actually *more* of a man for allowing yourself to feel the pain of your emotions and start a journey of healing. So, let it go Bro, so you can be the best version of yourself! Now, let's go to the throne of grace and if necessary, let our tears do the talking, shall we?

LET US PRAY

Abba Father, I thank You for being an emotional God. I thank You for being a God who was touched with our infirmities and understands everything we go through. You clothed Yourself in flesh and came to the earth to understand the frailty and complexities of man. Every emotion I have You lived You've felt, and because of this, Your compassion will never fail. Therefore, I can come to You boldly with how I'm feeling, not only when I'm happy but especially when I'm sad, angry, or confused.

Lord, I thank You for understanding every tear when I can't talk and every moan when I can't articulate how I'm feeling. I thank You for the tears I've sown, and I look forward to the harvest of joy that shall come as a result of them.
In Jesus' name, amen!

REFLECTION

When was the last time you had a good cry? What was it concerning? Reflect and record below.

God will not allow
a single tear to be
wasted.

I Have A Right to Celebrate!

NEHEMIAH 8:10 (NIV)

Do not grieve, for the joy of the Lord is your strength.

The book of Nehemiah is a story about a man on a quest to rebuild the walls and gates in Jerusalem after they had been destroyed for seventy years. By the eighth chapter, the walls in Jerusalem were rebuilt, and it was time to celebrate. Upon reading the laws of God, however, instead of celebrating, the people were sad and began to lament because they realized they fell and would fall short. Nehemiah encouraged the people to celebrate and to also take food to those who didn't have it. In the latter part of verse 10, he tells them not to grieve, for the joy of the Lord was their strength.

Most of us have broken areas in our lives. We have situations that we have yet to heal and be delivered from. If we are honest, there is that one thing (or a couple of things) that we've tried to put out of our minds as if it didn't happen, because it's too painful to deal with it. This may have been the plight of the people in Jerusalem. The trauma from being taken away into captivity and the vicious attacks that led to the destruction of the wall may have left those who returned with no hope, even after accomplishing a great task.

Have you been there? Have you ever tried to revisit a sore spot in your life and see how ruined it was? You just gave up on trying to clean up the rubble and broken pieces of the situation or even your heart? Have you ever just turned off your feelings because to rebuilding seemed way too painful? I understand all too well, but I also know that in order to move forward and be prepared for what God has for you in your future, you have to have the courage to go in, get rid of the broken and damaged pieces, and start rebuilding your life starting with your heart.

Once you get back on your feet after the ending of a relationship or a marriage, you'll find that things are way different. The way you move and operate in your singleness now is going to be much different, and you may feel like you fall short of what is expected of you now because of what you've been accustomed to. This is how the Jews felt once they heard the laws of God, but Nehemiah encouraged them, letting them know there was cause for celebration and that the joy of the Lord is and would be their strength.

So, friend, I say the same to you. You are working during these thirty-one days to rebuild that which was destroyed by circumstances. If you work hard, just like Nehemiah, it's not going to take as long as you think it will to be set free from the pain of your past. The walls of Jerusalem were ruined for seventy years, and it only took Nehemiah fifty-two days to rebuild! You may have been in the marriage for decades, broken for decades, angry for decades, sad for decades, but if you do the work, you can very well do the heart work and rebuild your life around in thirty-one days! When you finish rebuilding your life and put the gates on your heart, make sure you allow yourself to LIVE! Take your future by force, be grateful that you have the courage and fortitude to rebuild your life, and celebrate! Most importantly, someone is going to need your testimony. Someone is going to need to know that singleness is not a prison sentence, and being single again does not mean life, love, and the pursuit of happiness are unattainable. Someone is relying on you to rebuild and give them hope! Now, let's pray for the courage and strength to rebuild!

LET US PRAY

Heavenly Father, just as Nehemiah did, I come to You to do a survey of the ruins of my past. I ask that You accompany me on this quest to identify those areas that are broken and destroyed in my life. Help me to survey what remains in my past, and give me the tools and instruction on how to rebuild that which was destroyed. From self-esteem to self-love, I pray that You help me to rebuild those things that were torn down by people, past relationships, broken promises, or even by the words of my own mouth. Once I rebuild, my desire is to learn who I am and to rededicate myself to You.

Teach me how to navigate through this season in my life and celebrate my victory and my new season. Once I am healed and whole, grant me the courage to be able to tell my story in an effort to help someone else. I thank You for the opportunity to rebuild my life and live an abundant one.
In Jesus' name, amen!

REFLECTION

Make a list of your celebrations in your singleness thus far.
No celebration is too small!

Have the courage
to rebuild!

Authenticity with God

*Delight yourself in the Lord and he will give you
the desires of your heart.*

To delight in someone means to experience great pleasure in their presence and enjoy their company. This can only be done when you get to know a person; what they like, what they enjoy doing, what their love language is, and so on. This cannot be done between two strangers. In other words, you have to be in some sort of a relationship with the person in order to know the intimate details about them.

In Psalm 37:4, David is instructing us to delight ourselves in the Lord. As a single or single-again individual, this is paramount for daily living and complete happiness. In fact, here's a secret: learning how to delight yourself in the Lord will make you a better friend and spouse. There's no greater teacher to learn from when it comes to the topic of love than God. He is the ultimate example of love, both platonic and romantic. A man who delights himself in the Lord will know how to love, cherish and protect his wife. He will know how to effectively communicate and listen when she talks, even when she is long-winded. His relationship with God will transform him from a male to a man and from a man to a Kingdom man. When a man has a solid relationship with God, he will know when he is ready for a helpmate and not play any games in his quest to find her, and especially once he's found her.

A woman who delights herself in the Lord will know how to respect and support her husband. Her relationship with God will teach her submission and how to acquiesce and allow her husband to lead. A woman who delights herself in the Lord automatically transforms into a wife *before* she becomes one. She will know how to love on a deeper level and will know how to honor her husband in private and in public. A woman who has a solid relationship with the Lord will know the kind of king she wants because the King of kings has shown her the blueprint of what a kingdom man looks like. Knowing this, she will be able to recognize a king from a joker. A king is a godly *man* who is kingdom-driven. He's going to have purpose, a plan, and a plan for you. He's going to know where you fit in his life and will make provisions for you in his life. A king doesn't play games with your heart and wishes not to play games with your body. A joker, on the other hand, is a worldly *boy* who is not kingdom-driven. A joker plays games. He either flies by the seat of his pant when it comes to relationships or strategically says the things a woman wants to hear in order to win her mind and body while she loses her soul and ultimately ends up heartbroken.

Here's another fact: when you delight yourself in the Lord, He will give you the desires of your heart. Isn't that what the Word says? Now, here's the caveat. You can't fake a relationship with God just to get what you want. He knows everything. EVERYTHING. He knows our thoughts afar off, and He definitely knows our hearts. He also knows the timing and season in which He will release what He has for us to us, but we have to be ready, and a tell-tale sign of being ready is wrapping yourself so tightly in God that you lose track of time and your own desires. Your desires turn into God's desires, and you exchange your timeline for His divine timing.

This, my friend, is when God knows you are ready, and He can trust you with what He has for you. When God knows that He is the head and the most important thing in your life, He knows that you won't take the blessing and leave Him and lift up that person, relationship, or marriage as an idol and start to worship it. So, it behooves us to get in the presence of God, establish an authentic relationship with Him and while we wait for the blessings, learn all we can from God so we can be the best version of ourselves when we find or are found by the person we believe God for. Now, let us pray!

LET US PRAY

*Gracious and loving God, I come to You first with
a repentant heart, asking for Your forgiveness.
Forgive me for every time I approached Your throne
in prayer in order to get what I wanted. Forgive me
for wanting a romantic relationship or to be married
more than I wanted a relationship with You. Forgive
me for being angry with You because the marriage
didn't work. Forgive me for not trusting You with
my life and going before You, thinking I could do a
better job than You.*

*Father, I want to establish an authentic relationship
with You. I want to delight myself in You, not so You
can give me the desires of my heart, but because of
who You are. I want to learn from You the type of
husband/wife I am supposed to be. I want to be so
deep in You that when You send me who You have
for me, I'll know it's them, and they'll have to go
through YOU to get to ME. Until that time comes,
Lord, I want to know what love really is through
You. Teach me how to receive it AND how to give it.
I thank You, Lord, for this time of awakening, and I
look forward to having an intimate relationship with
You.
In Jesus' name, amen!*

REFLECTION

As with any relationship, there has to be planning and promises made of what two people will do to ensure they build a strong, loving, intimate foundation. God has already made His plans and promises concerning you. What are your plans for God?

You can't fake a
relationship with
God, just to get
what you want.

God is With Me

ISAIAH 41:10 (AMP)

Do not fear [anything], for I am with you; Do not be afraid, for I am your God. I will strengthen you, be assured I will help you; I will certainly take hold of you with My righteous right hand [a hand of justice, of power, of victory, of salvation].

One thing about a healthy relationship is the confidence you have. To know that you have a rock-solid foundation and someone in your corner who loves you, honors you, supports you and works *consistently* to make you happy and make your relationship work is everything. It is the dream of any single person who desires to be married one day, and it is the wish for the single again who desires to be married again.

Sometimes while we wait, it can get a little disheartening. You meet someone, they have potential, you never hear from them again. You meet someone, they have zero potential, and you wonder why they even approached you in the first place. Or, you meet someone, you invest time (months or sometimes years), money, emotions and you end up being left holding nothing but empty promises and a shattered heart.

But God! (look in the mirror and say to yourself, "BUT GOD!"). How wonderful is it to have a loving, powerful, protective God right there, assuring you that He's there with you? God is letting you know today that you don't have to fear. He knows your wants, needs, desires, dreams- He knows it all. He will always come through, always have your best interest at heart, always knows what's best for you, and will always make sure you have it. There's nothing like being in the center of God's will and in the palm of His hand. So, my friend, be confident that as you travel through this journey called singleness or single-again, God is with you.

LET US PRAY

Dear God. Thank You for always being there. Thank You for never leaving my side. Thank You for picking me up when I am down, strengthening me when I am weak, and holding onto me when I want to let go. Thank You for Your Word that assures me that You will always be there and You will never leave me. Your redemptive work on the Cross guarantees I can always, ALWAYS count on You. I decree and declare today that I am confident in my relationship with You and confident that I can lean and depend on You, no matter what is going on and how I am feeling.
I love You Lord, and I praise you,
in Jesus' name, amen!

REFLECTION

Write a break-up letter to fear. YES, to fear. This letter will serve as a reminder of the pain fear has caused and the reason you can no longer be yoked up with it.

_____

_____

_____

_____

_____

_____

_____

_____

_____

_____

_____

_____

_____

_____

There's nothing like being in the center of God's will and in the palm of His hand.

My Future Does Not Deserve My Past

PHILIPPIANS 3:13 (NLT)

*... Friends, don't get me wrong: By no means do
I count myself an expert in all of this, but I've got my
eye on the goal, where God is beckoning us onward to
Jesus. I'm off and running,
and I'm not turning back.*

We've been pretty honest on this journey, so it goes without saying that there are areas in our past that have dealt us some hard (but needful) lessons. There were some situations we've been tied up in, gotten ourselves into, and accepted into our lives that caused us to question the decisions we've made in the past. However, we have to understand that while those things may have caught us off guard, they didn't catch God by surprise. Again, let me remind you that God knew all we would go through, and He factored it all into the fabric of our lives.

Paul knew this all too well. He had a lot of history under his belt. Christian killer most notably – he coined himself as the "chief of all sinners." His conversion put him in a totally different place with a totally different mindset. With all that he did, he declared that his past was his past, and he was moving forward and not looking back. His relentless mindset to press forward to what God had for him is admirable. Paul shows us that no matter what we've done in our past, we can still move forward to our future.

And the same goes for you, my friend. Now, you're in a better place. You've unpacked all of your worries, emotions, past situations, and you've given them to God. You've forgiven and released those who hurt you and meant you harm. You've done the heart work to forgive yourself and be better in your single state. You won't have all of the answers because what need would there be for faith? However, what you do know you have to hold yourself accountable to:

There's a great future in store for you
God is the orchestrator of your future
You CANNOT look back

So, keep moving forward, my friend. Your past is your past, and your future does not deserve it. The man that God has for you does not deserve to pay for what the past did to you. That woman who you've been praying you find? She doesn't deserve the revenge you never gave to your past. That person who wants to be your friend? They don't deserve the petty shade and the cold shoulder your past dealt you. Your future doesn't deserve your past. Keep moving, keep healing, keep growing, press forward and DON'T LOOK BACK!

LET US PRAY

Heavenly Father, I thank You for being freed from my past. I recognize that everything I've been through has prepared me for this very moment. Every storm had a lesson in it, and my desire is to take those lessons and learn from them. I confess today that the past is the past, and my future doesn't deserve it. I want to be fair and faithful to my future, whether it be a new career, a friendship, or especially a spouse. Help me, God, to not pick up bad habits from my past and drag them into my future. Call out those negative traits that cannot go into my future. I won't look back but will do all I can in my power and by Your grace to keep pressing forward, and I thank You for helping me to do this. In Jesus' name, amen!

REFLECTION

List below all of the things you will **not** take into your future (i.e., low self-esteem).

_____

_____

_____

_____

_____

_____

_____

_____

_____

_____

_____

_____

_____

_____

Your future does not deserve your past.

Make Singleness Great!

Rejoice in the Lord always. I will say it again: Rejoice! Let your gentleness be evident to all. The Lord is near.

have a confession to make: the way singleness is portrayed in the world irritates me, and especially in the church. It bothers me, and it always has, even when I was married. You see, I didn't grow up in church, so I wasn't heavily influenced by church standards and man-made doctrines. I grew up learning to think for myself and make my own decisions. I went away to college, was able to travel and see the world and have a well-balanced life. Before I met my ex-husband, I had my own apartment, bank account, passport, and had been on quite a few vacations to the Caribbean, and already had my first experience of leaving the U.S. by myself. I always believed in not waiting for anyone to enjoy life or accomplish my goals.

This is by no means an indictment on any church or person and the way they were raised. People only know what they know, and my path was the path God carved out for me. I would be remiss if I didn't mention this hard topic because

I've been privy to conversations, and I've seen with my own eyes how people missed out on life because they were raised or led to believe that life doesn't begin until you are married. Particularly with women, the unspoken (or sometimes spoken) rule is you're not really a woman until a man counts you worthy of taking on his last name.

While this is happening, there are men who are not being taught how to be husbands while they are single. So, there are women prepared for marriage and men unprepared for marriage because men are not being held accountable on how to be husbands while they are still men, while the woman is expected to be a wife before she becomes one *(NOTE: In this regard, I'm talking about the woman preparing herself to be wife, not about giving a man wifey-privileges without the ring or official title).*

Why is this? Why are women rushing to be married and men going into marriage unadvisedly? I believe it's because we don't do singleness well, and that's because there hasn't been a solid, concrete foundation centered around singleness. For the most part, it's seen as a baseless, sexless, boring state that has absolutely no purpose. This couldn't be further from the truth.

Singleness is a wonderful time in a person's life. It's a time to get to know yourself, and all that concerns you, so you will be firm and confident in who you are before you meet that special someone. It's so important that, as singles, we show the world that there is nothing wrong with being single. We ought to be vibrant, happy, smiling, and rejoicing in the Lord! I'm not talking about putting on a façade when we are really feeling down. I'm talking about singleness and contentment being a lifestyle, and that lifestyle is centered in God and with God. There is always joy, peace, and happiness!

I will also add, singleness does not mean that your entire life, entire existence, every day, every single breath that you inhale and exhale is about Jesus, church, Bible study, prayer vigils, missionary work, prophetic utterances, long skirts, turtlenecks, speaking in tongues... need I go on?

LIVE!!

Please, know who you are OUTSIDE OF CHRIST. Yes, in Him we live, we move, and we have our being. Yes, without Him, we are nothing. Yes, we know all of those things... but what is your favorite color? What genre of movies do you like? What favorite book do you like to read besides the Bible? What kind of food do you like? Understanding who you are and what makes up the sum total of you will make your life so much more pleasant. When God created you, He created you with so many beautiful and wonderful things, and He breathed the breath of life into you for you to discover all of the greatness He put in you. So, live your life and discover all of who you are!

I encourage you, as you continue on in your relationship with the Lord, be happy that you're now in a place where you are willing to learn the sum total of who you are, recognize your worth, know where you are and who you belong to! Know that because you know these things and are discovering these things, you now can gain the confidence that you can be happy and single because YOU CAN BE HAPPY AND SINGLE! Let's make singleness great until THE LORD changes our status!

LET US PRAY

*Spirit of the true and living God, I come to say
thank You on today! Thank You for life, peace, joy,
and happiness! Thank You, Father, for leading
me to a place where I can rejoice where I am and
be genuinely happy about my life! I pray that You
continue to give me the grace to do those things that
may seem difficult to others, like traveling, dining,
and doing other fun activities alone. I pray, God,
that You place me around other like-minded singles
who want to enjoy their life as they wait for You
to release them into their next level in life. Lord,
continue to show me ways that I can enjoy my life
while also being a beacon of light and hope to those
who may not quite see singleness the way You would
want us to see it. Help me, as well as other singles,
to embrace this season with joy, understanding
that it is better to be single and happy temporarily
than to be married and miserable for a lifetime.
Thank You, Lord, for the remnant of singles You
are preparing to change the outlook on singleness. I
decree and declare I will rejoice in the Lord always
and be grateful for where I am and will be one of the
examples of those who make singleness a great thing!
In Jesus' name, amen!*

REFLECTION

Question: Who are you?

Caveat: You cannot use churchy jargon and scripture (i.e., I am a loving person, I am a great wife/husband in the making)

_____

_____

_____

_____

_____

_____

_____

_____

_____

_____

_____

_____

_____

_____

_____

Make Singleness Great!

I Lack Nothing!

1 TIMOTHY 6:6 (AMP)

But godliness actually is a source of great gain when accompanied by contentment [that contentment which comes from a sense of inner confidence based on the sufficiency of God].

believe, there is nothing more powerful, more captivating, and more intriguing than a woman (or man) who is content. Not only content in where they are in life, but confident in who they are. Now, what takes it to a whole different level, is when your contentment is nestled in God. This means that no matter where you are or what's happening around you, you have that inner confidence knowing God is the One who is in control of your life.

As a single person, to be completely confident and content where you are, is true godliness. It is the essence of what God requires because, at that point, He knows He can trust you with whatever He gives you. Godliness is being laser-focused on God. This doesn't mean you're in church all day every day, reading the Bible every single moment, or praying every hour on the hour. Though that is the warped expectation of singles, such is not the case.

Godliness with contentment is the amazing balance of being able to live a life in Christ and live in this world successfully. Yes, we are told we are sojourners traveling through this world and this is not our home. Yes, the Bible says to be in the world but not of it. But we still do live *in* the world. We have to live, breathe, earn income, pay bills, buy food, and while we do all of that, we can buy ourselves nice things, find and be found by love, enjoy the pleasures of intimacy once married, take trips, and a myriad of other wonderful things the Lord created for us to do as we travel through this life to our final heavenly destination.

Sufficiency is key in all of this. As a single person, you have to be confident that God truly is your source for everything. Since He is that source, everything you need is in Him. He has everything you need, including residence in that space in your heart while you actively wait in anticipation for the one who will take the place God is holding for him/her. So, rest in your godliness, walk in your contentment, take advantage of all you need from the all-sufficient One, and work that confidence, knowing that you are complete, whole, and lack nothing!

LET US PRAY

Heavenly Father, I thank You today for contentment. I thank You that through Your Word, You've given us the keys on how to live this life. I thank You on today for being content with where I am. I am confident that everything I've been through has prepared me for this moment in time. Thank You for showing me that I have no reason to worry or doubt who I am in You. Because You are the source of my everything, and because You are in control, I can stand confident in the fact that You have my entire life under control. Therefore, I can walk proudly and confidently in You, being assured that I am complete in who I am in this season in my life, and I lack nothing. No matter what is happening around me, no matter who is finding love, getting engaged, getting married, I am content where I am, knowing that what and who You have for me is for me, and it will not pass me by. I'm grateful for true godliness and contentment in You. In Jesus' name, amen!

REFLECTION

Question: Are you truly content in your singleness? Why or why not? (There's no wrong answer, only your honest feelings, and that is okay).

_____

_____

_____

_____

_____

_____

_____

_____

_____

_____

_____

_____

_____

_____

_____

Sufficiency is key.

Pray, Prepare & Position

ECCLESIASTES 4:12 (NLT)

A person standing alone can be attacked and defeated, but two can stand back-to-back and conquer. Three are even better, for a triple braided cord is not easily broken.

This is not only the end of the book, but it's the end of the chapter for this season in your life. No, I'm not saying you're going to pray today's prayer, write your reflection, close this book and then poof there is your spouse all of a sudden. What I am saying is, this is now the season for you to move from a place of dismal hopelessness and uncertainty to confidence and excitement about your future. Still, there is work to do, because mindsets and ways of thinking have to change. You want to set yourself up for success and there is one key factor I believe any single needs if they are going to be successful in finding/being found by their life partner.

If I can be honest, that one key factor was missing from all of my past relationships. It was the one thing that was needed but I didn't know it, and my ignorance cost me greatly every time. More often than not, I wondered why every relationship I was in never worked. Why was there always some type of betrayal, mistreatment, and ultimately loss where I was left holding my shattered heart? The reason why none of my relationships were successful was because the key component that was missing from them was God (duh!).

To be brutally honest, I don't remember a time where I prayed and asked God about a man or a spouse. It was so off my radar that when a guy approached me, I automatically took it to be God because I was not praying for a relationship, so I thought God was blessing me because I didn't make it a daily prayer because I wasn't thirsty for a man. While not being concerned about a relationship was good, not praying about the ones that surfaced was the problem. I accepted the guy with no questions asked until after the fact, and by that time, it was too late. Here's the caveat. Every single guy claimed **religion**. The problem was none of them had a **relationship**.

Often, the church talks about being equally or unequally yoked. While this is the absolute truth, I would venture to take it a step further and say being equally yoked is more than just two people being saved. Being equally yoked is having the same moral values, beliefs, and ideas about relationships. Being equally yoked is about being like-minded regarding goals, God, and specifically the things of God. Two people claiming to love Jesus is not enough. Equally yoked is specifically speaking to two people, but the third person (God) must be factored in. Two people can be equally yoked, but it's going to take God to keep that yoke from falling apart.

This is not mentioned in a lot of single settings, and a lot of singles are so busy wanting the relationship for companionship, personal and social media validation, they forget to pray earnestly, honestly about what they need as well as what they want. After the camera is off, the post is long gone, and the wedding and reception are a distant memory, two people have to live together and work their entire life to become one flesh.

The summation of my relationships left me in a place where I didn't want to be bothered anymore. I had written my life off to one of ministry, business, legacy building for my children, and lots of travel. That was going to be what my life looked like and I grew to be okay with that. However, I remember the prophetic word I received and the subsequent ones after that. Those words kept playing in my mind and pulling at the strings of my heart, because while I had given up on the possibility of love, God had not, and had it factored in still after all of the incredibly foolish decisions I made in my past. So, one day, I decided to lay my will (which was rooted in fear and disappointment) down, and do the courageous thing and open up my heart to the possibility of love and being found by and loved by a man who God had for me. I put together a plan of what I would do according to God's word and that plan was to Pray, Prepare and Position myself for my next season. I invite you today, to do the same.

Pray

This can sometimes be the hardest part, because you can't go to God in prayer not believing for what you are praying for. So, you have to have an honest conversation with the Father and tell Him how you really feel at the onset. After you release those fears, start praying to God and begin to believe. Let your prayers be very specific in what you desire according to God's will. When I started this journey, after a while, my prayers became more like a dialogue between God and I, and I started to get answers to questions I had concerning my past, and those answers would help me in my future.

Prepare

The preparation period is an ongoing process, but the most important thing is to begin preparing, and that's where singles (in my opinion) go wrong. As I said in a previous chapter, you can't prepare to be a wife once you have the ring, and you can't prepare to be a husband once you've said, "I do." Preparation comes long before a potential mate even shows up. Can you cook? Do you cook? How's your credit? How's your relationship with your family? How are your communication skills? How do you respond or react to bad news or disagreements? Has anything happened in your past that would warrant you needing to seek counseling or therapy? *Have you been to counseling or therapy?* These are some of the questions you need to ask yourself as you wait for your season to change.

Position

While you are tackling those questions and preparing yourself, it's important to position yourself for your future. This can look like many different things. Having gone through this 31-day devotional is one way. Scrubbing your social media pages of photos and videos that do not put you in a good light is another. Changing the type of people you hang around, is definitely a huge factor. Ladies, are all of your friends single, chatty, catty, and miserable? Do they spend more time talking about who's dating who and who's not happy than they do working on themselves? Are they out in the club every weekend? And men, is the company you keep about smashing and playing video games all day? Do they refer to women as queens or do they use derogatory terms to refer to women? Are they kingdom men looking for kingdom women to grow and build with, or are they just out here in these streets acting like jokers? Know your circle and who dwells among you. Your environment can very well cause you to miss out on God's best for you. Position yourself around people who are going to challenge you to be a better you for you, and your future.

By no means am I saying I have all of the answers. These tools are just a fraction of the exhaustive list of things one can do to prepare themselves for their future. The running theme in all of this is that God is in the midst. When you pray, you're praying to God. When you prepare, God is showing you those things you need to fix. When you position, God will show you who you need to release out of your life, who you need to allow in, and who you need to strategically place yourself around for the sake of your present and future. You want God to be the foundation, the center, the glue, and the mediator in your relationship. I don't know what your future holds, but I know Who holds it, and I pray that the next season will be your very best season and that you come into the fullness of what have been and are praying for. Let us pray.

LET US PRAY

Heavenly Father, I thank You for this 31-day journey. I thank You for the hard conversations, the convictions, and perhaps the difficulties I've had to tread through. As I close this chapter and get ready for my next, I thank You for strategically and divinely setting me up for success. I pray, God, that You give me the courage to hope again, and the fortitude to put my courage into action and do what is needed so I can be the best version of myself. God, I invite You into this next season in my life and pray that You take up permanent residence in my life forever. I pray for my future spouse, that they are learning the same tactics and principles You have given me. I pray that You heal and protect the person You have for me and that You deliver them from all past hurts, disappointments and traumas.

You are omniscient and omnipresent, so I know because You sit up high and look down low, You are simultaneously working on both of us to create the best version of ourselves so we can be that to one another. So, until that time God, I pray that You continue to work on me. I decree and declare that I am the clay in Your hands, and I will allow You as the Master Potter to mold me and shape me into a beautiful piece of art, as You mold my spouse into a wonderful masterpiece. It is in Your mighty name I pray, amen.

REFLECTION

Continue this prayer. Write out your own prayer for your spouse as you wait, if you desire to be married (or be married again). If your desire is not marriage, write down any last thoughts you have about this journey.

Pray.
Prepare.
Position.

About the Author

Stacy Y. Thomas is the youngest and only girl of 3 children and the proud mother of two beautiful little girls. Born and raised in the projects in The Bronx, NY, Stacy gave her life to Christ at the tender age of 11. She worked hard to get out of the "P.J.'s" and in July of 1993 left The Bronx to attend Syracuse University in Syracuse, NY. After obtaining her degree in Fashion Design from S.U., she fulfilled her life-long dream of becoming a licensed Cosmetologist. After years in corporate America, she decided to start her own natural hair and skin care line I Design Beauty, LLC.

Stacy knew there had to be more than just giving her life to Christ and being "saved." In the Spring of 2001, she joined Morning Star Full Gospel Assembly, Bronx, NY and served faithfully under in many ministries, and many capacities including Assistant Director of the Christian Drama Guild; Young Adult Choir, Dance Ministry, and as a Sunday School Teacher (just to name a few). In August of 2008, Stacy heard the call of God to preach the unadulterated gospel of Jesus Christ and started her journey. It wasn't an easy feat, and Stacy experienced many hardships along the way, including a near death experience on her way home from a business trip in Hong Kong, where she suffered a bowel obstruction mid flight, and had to have emergency surgery to save her life. This life-altering experience was confirmation the devil was determined to stop the plan of God, and she was determined to make him into the liar he is.

Out of the ashes of sickness, calamity and life lessons from the school of hard knocks, another passion within Stacy began to burn, which was writing. As her marriage began to unravel, she started to release her feelings by journaling. In her first book *"Where Do I Go from Here? Redefining Yourself After Heartbreak and Brokenness"* (released August 2, 2016), Stacy pens the tools and tactics she used to go from brokenness to being made whole and living an abundant life following a divorce.

After 11 years, Stacy answered the call of God on Sunday, August 18, 2019, becoming a licensed minister at Morning Star Full Gospel Assembly, where the current Senior Pastor is Rubin S. Thompson. She is a part of the Ecclesiastical staff, serves on the Women's Fellowship Committee Board, and is the Director of The Children of Holiness, which is a praise dance ministry for the youth ages 7-17, as well as the Liturgical Dance Ministry, which is a praise dance ministry for adults ages 18 & up.

With her professional career, entrepreneurial spirit, ministry duties; as a saved, Holy Ghost filled divorced mother of two beautiful, young ladies, Stacy believes Romans 8:28 says it best, *"And we know that in all things God works for the good of those who love him, who have been called according to his purpose."*

Facebook: Stacy Y. Thomas
Instagram: @iamstacy.t
Website: www.iamstacyt.com

9 781948 877855